Raising a Successful Child in America:

A Black Perspective

Raising a Successful Child in America: A Black Perspective

By Alphonso Williams

ISBN: 978-1-7359531-0-6 (Paperback)
ISBN: 978-1-7359531-1-3 (eBook)

Cover design by pro_ebookcovers
Edited by Porsché Mysticque Steele and Corey Lewis

Acknowledgments

I'd like to thank my family for their support and encouragement during this project. I would especially like to thank my maternal grandparents, Mathew and Ann Williams, for raising me during my formative years and teaching me the importance of patriotism, and for laying a foundation of personal ethics. I would like to thank my paternal grandparents Samuel and Martha Watts for always stressing the importance of personal responsibility and talking about the possibilities of America. I would also like to thank my in-laws Allen and Mary Foster.

The love and encouragement I received from these folks helped mold me into who I became and helped set my value and belief systems in place. My mom and stepdad Mary Armistead-Reynolds and William Armistead Jr. taught me to see the possibilities in everything and to not accommodate failure. Sometimes it was hard to see the world through rose-colored glasses. Ultimately, I'm glad that this paradigm was pushed onto my young psyche.

I would also like to acknowledge with a special thanks to Tae Kwon Do Master Hwa Chong. He always encouraged me and chided me when he thought I was being a quitter.

The love and encouragement I receive from my wife Debra and children Matthew and Brandee pave the way to a future of our own choosing. Without them, I am just a leaf blowing in the wind.

And a special thank you to…

Corey Lewis. Without your tough commentary and spot-on editing, I could not have gotten this far with this book project. Porsché Steele your timely insights and opinions kept me writing when I wanted to stop and just throw in the towel.

Guys, your help is greatly appreciated.

Summary

An uplifting track for American parents, intended to encourage sound parenting techniques so that *ALL* American children will be positioned to prosper by taking advantage of American ideals and opportunities. There is an underlying theme of advancing the cause of national unity and the possibility of inclusive prosperity.

Contents

1. Introduction and Why

I don't consider myself to be smarter or better than anyone else. It's just that I've been successful in raising my own children to become productive and financially stable members of society. I've also observed other parenting styles that have appeared to yield less successful results.

The examples and evidence I refer to in the book are not just anecdotal but backed by expert research and studies listed throughout the book. This book is not just for African American families, it is for everyone and anyone who wishes the best for their children and is interested in exploring different ideas about how to accomplish that. My reasons for writing this book are varied. I have observed that here in America the African-American segment of the populace which currently sits at more than 12% of the population seems to be stuck and face difficulties when striving for the American dream; so much so that some may not strive for it at all. It seems that we are not translating our parents and grandparents' values and examples of generational perseverance to the younger generation.

Let's start with some basic truths,

Basic Truth #1 - Parents should want their kids to be successful. By successful, I mean being happy, financially stable, having high moral values, being civic-minded, healthy (mentally and physically), and trustworthy.

Basic Truth #2 - What's good for Black America *is good for America*. African American culture is the trendsetter here in America. It has been for hundreds of years. Everything from cooking styles like southern cooking, clothing, hairstyles, greetings like the fist-bump and the high five, media norms, television shows, movies, and music. There's no question that African-Americans have helped shape America.

Basic Truth #3 - It's time for African Americans to take their place as *leaders* in finance, wealth generation, money management, and business development.

Basic Truth #4 - In America, nothing worthwhile is given to you. Everything must be earned. It is *unpatriotic* to raise our children in such a way that they can't access the American Dream.

"The world craves creativity, individuality, and successful methods. Supply a waiting world with these needs, and it will beat a path to your door. Black America this is your responsibility!"

- Excerpt from Think and Grow Rich - A Black Choice: Dennis Kimbro and Napoleon Hill

Basic Truth #5 - Time keeps marching on! Don't procrastinate, don't put off what you know has to be done. Whether we take an active role in trying to guide our children to success or sit back and watch life just happen, time still moves on!

Basic Truth #6 - The story of African Americans is *American* history!

Basic Truth #7 - Getting pregnant is *never* an accident. Merriam-Webster defines an accident as an *unforeseen* and unplanned event or circumstance. Humans procreate by having sex. Our children are never accidents, you must think of them as blessings made from love.

Google search defines the American Dream as the idea that every U.S. citizen has an equal opportunity to achieve success and prosperity through hard work, determination, and initiative.

From a more basic perspective, the key aspects of the American dream are the feeling of being financially sound, and safe within your home and neighborhood. Being able to afford decent transportation. The reality of sending your kids to college for a great educational experience, and vacationing with the family. Enjoying life and living as stress-free as possible. I think most people consider these things to be a big part of the American dream. This is why we have so many foreign-born people coming to access this land of opportunity, taking a chance on the American dream. We have to make sure all our children can access the American Dream as well.

The Founding Fathers of our country understood the importance of this dream. The following excerpt from the Declaration of Independence says it all,

"We hold these truths to be self-evident, that all men are created equal, that they are endowed by their Creator with unalienable *Rights*, that among these are *Life*, *Liberty* and the pursuit of *Happiness*."

The possibility of achieving the American dream is even more so a reality today than it was at the time of our countries founding. The pursuit of this dream is open to men as well as women, all ethnic and racial classes, also the rich and the poor. By raising our children correctly, we can greatly improve their welfare and happiness, now and into the future.

America is an awesome place to live when you have discretionary income. Living in America can suck when or and if you don't have the necessary financial resources to prosper. I've been poor and I've been middle class. Having a discretionary income is a much better way to live in America.

As parents, we should do our best to teach our children how to strive rather than settling for less. I can still hear my grandfather and my stepfather constantly drilling into me this phrase, *"Al, it is your responsibility to do better and go farther than I did."*.

It is my hope that this book not only helps black families and their children but helps all of America. As trendsetters for America, I hope that African Americans and will take their place as examples of civic duty, patriotism, and national pride. In order to strengthen these ideals as a nation, we must get back to a sense of unity and a sense of family. The ideals of unity and family start with our children.

Our nation has proven time and time again that in times of crisis we *always* come together. Whether it's during acts of war, terrorism, natural disasters, or economic collapse - Americans bleed blue (the blue of our flag stands for vigilance, perseverance, and justice). We must help our children strive for success, which will in turn strengthen our families. This will directly and positively impact and strengthen America.

I know it's a cliché but it's true - "United we stand divided we fall.". When the World Trade Center was destroyed during the 911 attack, the terrorists didn't stop the planes and let any ethnic or racial group leave. No, they were out to kill Americans, *all* Americans! The attempt was to strike fear into the American Dream. A funny thing happened though; the opposite response occurred. American Unity shone through brighter than ever. For almost a year the media reported a sharp decrease in sectarian politics. In many ways, our country was more united than it had ever been.

Raising a new generation of smart, independent, and financially stable children will go a long way in helping the country become unified and *staying* unified.

African Americans are a true melting pot. Our bloodline heritage is African, Caucasian, Hispanic, Asian, Native American, and many others. As such we have inherited from our forefathers the strengths and abilities that have made the whole American experience possible. All we need to do is exercise these abilities as we strive toward success. Let's "Pull **ourselves** up by our own bootstraps!".

As you take your journey through this book there will be some things that you will not agree with. I ask that you keep an open mind and not disregard them without thinking about the whys and how's. This book is not so much a road map, but a conversation starter to get the mental juices flowing.

Use this book as a workbook. Highlight areas that are of help to you. Write notes in the margins if and when a passage brings back one of your own memories that may help your child. My hope is that this book gets the reader out of their comfort zones and helps them take some action. Our children are worth it.

I am not a clinical expert or a child psychologist. What I am is a father who loves his children, and I've been blessed to be able to raise two successful black children here in America with the help of my wife and family. If you only get one idea from this book that helps you raise your child then this book was worth it.

2. Love Foundation

Above all, love each other deeply, because love covers over a multitude of sins.

- 1 Peter 4,8

As parents, our most important job is to guide our children *safely* into adulthood. We teach them how to be constructive members of society, and how to be able to establish and *maintain* loving relationships and bonds with others. If we can do that, everything else is the icing on the cake.

Love and affection are universal. Even when we observe animals in nature, we see animal parents showing love and affection to their offspring. Our pets cozy up to us and really appreciate our affections. If our pets cherish and benefit from our love and affection, how much more will our children benefit from our love and affection?

Rearing children takes real work and effort. If done correctly the bonds of love you build with your children will enhance your life immensely. A lot of us probably have no idea where to start when it comes to raising children.

"Start where you are. Use what you have. Do what you can."

- Arthur Ashe

Start by dealing with your children through a spectrum of love. If you have any feelings of resentment toward your children while they are still minors, figure out a way to get rid of those feelings. It is not the child's fault that they were born! Nor is it their fault that the other parent may not be supportive of you or your children. It is not the child's fault for the financial circumstances you may find yourself in. Feelings of resentment can and will sabotage any healthy relationships that you try to establish with your kids. Children instinctively know if they are truly loved or if their parents are just going through the motions. Just remember, the past is the past and no one can go back and change the past. All we can do is control the here and now hoping for the best moving forward.

Thinking of our children as a blessing and not a burden helped sustain us through the trials of parenthood. Also, the universe seemed to open up and bless my family both spiritually and financially when we had another mouth to feed.

I believe strongly in this concept that children are a blessing. This is directly related to the concept of the power of positive thinking. The benefits of positive thinking have been explored so often that there is no need to further explain it here. I will simply state that this phenomenon of positive thinking can and will have positive influences on our relationships.

A few years later, I discussed this phenomenon with my friend Walter McGuire Jr. and he put it in perspective. He said that "as a *good* and *loving* parent when faced with another mouth to feed, the right attitude will help you creatively figure out how to make things happen." When you truly love your children, you will move mountains and figure out ways to make it happen!

I've observed that families who truly love each other and not just tolerate each other have kids who are mentally strong, better problem solvers, and also seem more socially well rounded.

"Children's children are a crown to the aged, and parents are the pride of their children"

- Proverbs 17,6

No matter what our children's personalities are, they are still our children. If you hate your children and can't wait for them to become adults and move out, you may be setting yourself up for failure. Let's not fool ourselves. As parents, we would love to have healthy loving relationships with our adult children and grandchildren. But it has to start while our children and grandchildren are young. The older I get the more important these familial bonds become.

If you have a strained relationship with a teenager or adult child and there are feelings of resentment on both sides that have existed for years. Chances are that this relationship could be strained for years to come or worse without some serious fence-mending.

If you do find yourself in a tense relationship with your children or grandchildren and you're not happy about it, try to start over. When you are trying to overcome these awkward relationships and hurts from the past it is important to be patient. It takes work to repair relationships. It is not an overnight process, but **with time, effort, and understanding** these relationships can be mended and become stronger than ever.

My mother was a no-nonsense parent who at times could be emotionally detached, but we knew that she loved us, because she constantly told us and put our needs ahead of her own. Growing up I thought that my mother was the meanest woman in the world and didn't want me to have any friends. As I got older and had my own family, I developed a deeper appreciation for what she had to go through to help my siblings and I arrive at adulthood.

"Love is patient, love is kind. It does not envy, it does not boast, it is not proud. It does not dishonor others, it is not self-seeking, it is not easily angered, it keeps no record of wrongs. Love does not delight in evil but rejoices with the truth. It always protects, always trusts, always hopes, always perseveres. Love never fails."

- 1 Corinthians 13,4-8

I ran across this wonderful article on Motherly (the site is www.mother.ly) written by Mark Oliver. It was so good I had to include it here...

The Most Important Thing Children Need Is Just Love
By Mark Oliver

"He needs to toughen up."

It's a line we've all heard more than once – sometimes from grandparents, from friends, or even from ourselves. We watch our children grow and we worry. We imagine them alone at school or moving out on their own and wonder how they'll hold up when we're not there to protect them.

We want our kids to be wildly successful adults, and so we spend our time worrying about the right way to discipline them, the right way to encourage them – the right way to manage every minute of our lives around them.

In the end, though, the thing that matters the most is love. Whether you use the newest parenting techniques or trust the old wisdom, your children will grow up well so long as you love them.

Parents who touch, talk, and play with their kids, who are patient with them, and reassure them when they're worried make great kids every time.

That's not just sentiment – it's fact. Parenting research has proven time and time again loving your children is the one thing that makes all the difference – in so many important ways.

Love makes a child's brain grow.

From the very beginning, your love for your children affects how they develop. Your child's growth has to do with more than just the food they eat and the exercise they get – love affects it, too.

Researchers looked at how well mothers supported their children when they tried to do a difficult task, and then checked back about 5 years later to do a brain scan. The more supportive the mothers were, the more the child's brain – specifically the hippocampus – had grown.

This part of the brain controls how kids learn, how much they can remember, and how they handle stress. Children that are supported by their parents when they struggle, get more than just a little help – they get bigger brains.

Supporting your children improves their self-esteem.

Sometimes, it's tempting to raise a self-reliant child. We want our kids to be strong on their own so that they can learn how to believe in themselves. If they handle their problems on their own, we might imagine, they'll get stronger.

It turns out, though, a child's self-esteem really comes down to how much their parents support them. A study on middle schoolers found that the more kids felt their parents supported them, the stronger their self-esteem was. In particular, this had a big impact on girls, who need that external support just a little bit more.

As long as we believe in our kids, they'll copy us – and they'll believe in themselves.

Parental warmth makes healthier kids.

Loving your kids doesn't just make them smarter and more confident – it even makes them healthier. One study sought to find out how childhood abuse led to heart problems later in life.

What they found, though, was that it wasn't just abuse that affected kids' health – it was every little bit of love.

The more children felt like their parents gave them warmth and affection, the healthier the kids were when they grew up. Even when a child has been abused, their risk of cardiovascular diseases, cholesterol issues, heart disease, stroke, and diabetes will go down – as long as they're given a loving home.

Believing in your children improves their grades.

We try a lot of different things to help our kids succeed. We might fill them up with extracurriculars to strengthen their minds or lighten their load to let them focus on school.

We might push them to work hard on their homework or encourage them to let out some of that stress.

The thing that really makes the difference, though, is just believing that they can do it.

A study looked at how much parents believe their children can succeed, and found it made a huge difference.

When they followed up a few years later, the kids whose parents consistently believed in their abilities earned significantly higher grades – an average, 0.21 higher GPA – than their less supported peers.

So, try whatever parenting styles you feel you need to try. But remember, as long as you show your kids that you believe in them, as long as you offer them love, warmth, affection, and support, your kids are going to be just fine.

- Mark Oliver

Please kiss and hug your children, and not just when they are babies. These little displays of affection will mean a lot to your children. The **lack** of them when I was growing up sure didn't help me any.

My brother-in-law, Larry, struggled with drug addiction and suffered from explosive bouts of aggression later in life. He would have been considered a failed parent by any stretch of the imagination, but he got a few important things right when it came to parenting. Once he told me, "Look here bro, you can't be scared to hug and kiss your kids. You better do it while you have a chance, you don't know what tomorrow brings."

Thanks to my crazy brother-in-law I became a hugger. Hugging is contagious. Now that my mom is older, she too has become a hugger. We've even turned my son-in-law into a hugger. Showing affection enhances the human experience.

On those days when you have a million things going on and you find yourself so stressed that it feels like your head will explode any second, stop what you are doing and find your child or children. Hug them and tell them that you love them! Not only will they like it, but it will also make you feel a hundred times better and help alleviate stress.

Our kids may disappoint us or make us angry but offer them your love unconditionally anyway. At the end of the day, you **must** find a way to love your kids and make sure that they know that you love them. Love them with all that you have because we really don't know what tomorrow may bring.

3. Get Some Help

The African proverb that says, "It takes a village to raise a child." is absolutely spot on. Especially with the information overload currently in full swing, it is almost impossible to raise your child on your own. If nothing else, when you are at your wit's end and totally stressed out and ready to kill your kids, having that someone available to temporarily take the kids and give you a sanity break can mean everything to you.

"None of us got where we are solely by pulling ourselves up by our bootstraps. We got here because somebody - a parent, a teacher, an Ivy League crony or a few nuns - bent down and helped us pick up our boots."

- Thurgood Marshall

Most times, our parent's and grandparents' experiences can help us raise our children. Try sharing with your children some of the positive and inspirational experiences and stories passed down from previous generations, they can have a big impact. When my son got discouraged about schoolwork and wanted to take a break from college. I was able to remind him of my Grandpa's school experience and it helped turn him around and appreciate the situation that he was in.

Set up a network of people that you **trust**. The keyword here is trust. Please don't try to pawn your kids off to just anyone. I know that this seems like common sense, but the headlines beg to differ. There are too many instances when children have been abused physically and or mentally because they had been entrusted with someone that wasn't trustworthy. Let's not compound the challenges our children will face by giving them unnecessary baggage to have to overcome.

Keep an open dialog with your children. By keeping an open-door policy with your children, if a situation arises and someone attempts to harm your children, you'll know about it. Your children will be open to sharing their fears and hurts with you.

If a situation arises and your child tells you that something improper has occurred. Please *believe* your child until proven otherwise! _Don't_ automatically assume that your child is lying. You owe it to your children to at least investigate any charge of impropriety, no matter how unlikely or outlandish an allegation may seem to be.

During your investigation check for any marks or bruises etc. If need be, take your child to a physician to be checked out. Above all else, don't argue at or berate your child about the situation.

While getting help from others with our child-rearing, please keep your guard up when it comes to your children. Impropriety can come from any source. It could be a favorite aunt, uncle, stepmother, stepfather, kindly neighbors, church friends, work friends, acquaintances from the mosque or temple, your childhood friends, etc. My goal here is not to make you paranoid, but to make sure that you are watchful and aware of what could happen.

Another important area of help for younger children is in preschool and early childhood education. Pre-Kindergarten educational help is critical for your child's long-term academic success.

> *The research evidence supports the contention that better-quality childcare is related to better cognitive and social development for children.*

> *While these effects of childcare quality are in the modest to moderate range, they are found even after adjusting for family selection factors related to both the quality of care and to children's outcomes. Numerous studies have found short-term effects of childcare quality on children's cognitive, social, and emotional development during the preschool years. Longer-term effects lasting into the elementary school years have also been found, although fewer longitudinal studies have been conducted to examine this issue.*

> *Moreover, these results indicate that the influences of childcare quality are important for children from all backgrounds. While some studies have found even*

stronger effects for children from less advantaged backgrounds (suggesting that this issue may be even more critical for children already at greater risk for school failure) the findings indicate that children from more advantaged backgrounds are also influenced by the quality of care.

As a whole, these findings suggest that policies which promote good quality childcare during the preschool years are important for all children. Other research suggests that good quality care is expensive to provide; it is associated with well-trained and educated staff, low staff-child ratios, low staff turnover rates, good wages, and effective leadership. Given the high cost as well as the relative paucity of good-quality care, consideration needs to be given to both the availability and the affordability of care. The most successful policies will need to take all these factors into account, so that good quality care is a realistic option for all children. Given the high usage rates of childcare during the preschool years, such an investment would seem to be an important path to explore in improving children's readiness for and success in school.

`Ellen S. Peisner-Feinberg, PhD

FPG Child Development Institute, University of North Carolina at Chapel Hill, USA
February 2007, 2nd ed.

Again, I want to reiterate that there is not someone behind every corner that wants to harm your child. Most folks are what they seem to be, just be aware and practice really listening to your children. This ability to really listen to your children will head off most problems and highlight anything that is not quite right.

If you are given child-rearing advice that you don't necessarily agree with; remember to please be polite, but you shouldn't implement any advice that you don't agree with. As long as that advice was offered through true sincerity, please respond in kind.

"When we give cheerfully and accept gratefully, everyone is blessed."

- Maya Angelou

Usually, some of the best places to get child-rearing help are from our parents, grandparents, or other family members that have real-world experience. Their life experiences could be invaluable in helping shape your child. When sharing these experiences with your children make sure that there is an objective or lesson behind the story. Discuss with your children modern examples of how to implement these lessons.

If your parents or grandparents are not available or living a lifestyle not conducive to your values then try parental support groups, parenting classes, parenting magazines, religious organizations outreach programs, parenting blogs, etc.

There is a ton of information out there, but it has to be vetted using *your* value system, regardless of where the information comes from including this book. Make sure that any advice taken meets your value system. If something doesn't feel right in your gut, ***don't*** do it. Also, don't be paralyzed by inaction and indecision. If you need help, find it! If you want advice, get it! Do not put your head in the sand, do something.

"The best way to not feel hopeless is to get up and do something. Don't wait for good things to happen to you. If you go out and make some good things happen, you will fill the world with hope, you will fill yourself with hope."

\- Barack Obama

---

4. Control Your Children's Environment

Control as much of your child's environment as you can. This means not just controlling the friends he or and she hangs around, but also controlling their television viewing, books read, video game time, etc. We need to control anything negative that may influence our children. If your child is into video games then monitor the games they play. Don't buy them or let your child play excessively violent games or games that promote criminal behavior.

Do not be misled, Bad company corrupts good character.

- 1 Corinthians 15,33

When I worked in I.T. we had the term "GIGO". It means 'garbage in garbage out'. If our children are constantly being assaulted by unhealthy input into their developing psyches what other outcomes can we expect but damaged personalities and unhealthy mental states?

Your child's environment is so important to their development, look at what the US National Library of Medicine and the National Institutes of Health have to say...

Mental illnesses produce some of the most challenging health problems faced by society, accounting for vast numbers of hospitalizations, disabilities resulting in billions in lost productivity, and sharply elevated risks for suicide. Scientists have long known that these potentially devastating conditions arise from combinations of genes and environmental factors. Genetic research has produced intriguing biological insights into mental illness, showing that particular gene variations predispose some individuals to conditions such as depression and schizophrenia.

Now, thanks to a growing union of epidemiology and molecular biology, the role of the environment in the etiology of mental illness has become clearer. Indeed, E. Fuller Torrey, president of the Treatment Advocacy Center, a nonprofit organization that promotes treatment advances in psychiatry, suggests that mental illnesses increasingly fall into the realm of environmental health. And from that platform, he says, new treatment advances could soon emerge.

"Some of the greatest advancements in twentieth-century medicine were achieved by identifying and preventing infectious diseases through vaccination, improved sanitary measures, improved nutrition, and diminished hazards of environmental contaminants," adds Alan Brown, an associate professor of clinical

psychiatry and epidemiology at Columbia University Medical Center. "If environmental risk factors for [mental illness] can be validated and confirmed, there is every reason to expect they will point to preventive measures that lower their risks and morbidity."

Scientists define "environment" in the realm of mental illness broadly, some going so far as to suggest it encompasses everything that isn't an inherited gene. That's a departure from traditional thinking in environmental health, however, which has historically viewed environmental threats in the context of infectious agents, pollutants, and other exogenous factors that influence the individual's physical surroundings.

Environmental threats to mental health include these traditional parameters—along with pharmaceutical and illicit drugs, injuries, and nutritional deficiencies—but also consist of psychosocial conditions that relate to the individual's perceptions of the social and physical world.

Any number of circumstances—for instance, sexual abuse, falling victim to crime, or the breakup of a relationship—can produce psychosocial stress. But experts assume each of these circumstances triggers more primal reactions, such as feelings of loss or danger, which serve to push victims toward a particular mental state. "Feelings of pure loss might lead to depressive disorders, while feelings of pure danger might lead to anxiety disorders," explains Ronald Kessler, a professor of health care policy at Harvard Medical School. "And feelings of loss and danger might lead to both simultaneously." Either alone or in combination, psychosocial and physiological stressors can interact with genetic vulnerability to alter brain chemistry and thus alter the individual's mental health.

Several lines of evidence point to an environmental role in psychiatric disease. Among identical twins, if one becomes schizophrenic, the risk to the other is on average less than 50%, suggesting that environmental influences must somehow be involved. Similar findings have been observed with depression and other mental disorders.

Charles W. Schmidt
Environ Health Perspect. 2007 Aug; 115(8), A404–A410.
oi, 10.1289and ehp.115-a404
PMCID, PMC1940091 PMID, 17687431

Even though we can't pick our children's friends, to a large degree we can control who they hang around with. The old adage "you are who you hang around" seems to be truer today than ever before. Attempt to surround your children with individuals who have complementary value systems that align with your own.

Walk with the wise and become wise, for a companion of fools suffers harm.

\- Proverbs 13,20

For example, if the neighbors down the street are always fighting or arguing and it spills over outside for the whole neighborhood to see. You might want to discourage your child from hanging out at that home and offer alternatives.

When I was fifteen my mother tried to discourage me from hanging out at a neighbor's home because of the atmosphere there. My friend's mother wanted to be friends with her teenage kids, so she looked the other way when kids hanging out at their home smoked and drank. From a teenager's perspective, this house was exciting and had it going on. There was drinking, smoking, and girls hanging out there. My mother spoke to me about hanging out there but offered no alternatives. Her conversation went something like this

"Al, I know those girls are letting you do whatever you want to do, but that lifestyle will lead you to nothing but trouble."

My reply at the time was, "Momma I got this. This is big Al; I know what I'm doing."

Of course, I didn't know anything, I didn't have enough life experience at fifteen to know what I didn't know. My mom tried talking, punishments, threats, etc. Nothing worked. As soon as that punishment was over, I would run right back over there. It got so bad that after I had a run-in with our landlord, my mother made me move out.

I was able to move in with my mom's god-daughter (Darlene) and her boyfriend. My Mom's god-daughter was only four years older than I was at the time and was just starting out. She had limited furniture and no refrigerator. But she had a big heart and let me move in rent-free.

Around that time, I had found a job at the Cass Tech Night School thanks to one of my teachers Mr. Simons (spelling?). I was exposed to the wonderful world of having and earning my own money. I earned a whopping $2 per hour working 12 hours per week. Thank God for this job. After taxes, I netted $45 every two weeks from that job. The job helped me to improve my study habits. Also allowed me to eat! Though my god-sister opened her home to me she couldn't offer any financial support, and I was too stubborn to allow my mother to help me. I had to figure out practical things like food and transportation since I didn't attend the neighborhood high school. I went to high school downtown. God provided me with the answer. Soup was nonperishable, no refrigeration needed.

At that time, Campbell's condensed soup was less than 50 cents a can. I promptly purchased 24 cans of assorted Campbell's soup, a large box of saltine crackers, and two cans of chili. For breakfast, I stopped at

Gasman's Liquor store every morning and purchased an orange drink (imitation orange juice), and a pack of cheese and peanut butter crackers. Problem solved.

Lunch was provided in school and I had soup at night, I supplemented my food intake with chili on the weekends. School provided me bus tickets to travel back and forth to school.

When I moved out, my mom allowed me to take my bedroom furniture and my clothes. For entertainment, all I had was an A.M. transistor radio. You would have thought that since I could now come and go as I pleased that I would have been totally out of control, but just the opposite happened. Since I didn't have much extra money anymore. I sure missed my allowance! I had to find activities that were free and would keep me out of trouble. I've always been afraid of going to prison thanks to my uncle Paul. He graphically told me the truth about prison life from his own experience. The beatings, stabbings, rapes, lack of decent meals, no female company, and the loneliness. I wanted no part of that!

I found that the main library was awesome and free. The museums were free or almost free to students. Once in a while, I was also able to catch a kung fu movie at the Fox Theatre for $1 at that time. I started filling my free time with these activities. I slowly stopped hanging out with my so-called friends. They didn't want to hang out where I wanted to hang out! A few of them ended up going to jail and being investigated by the FBI for various crimes committed across state lines.

Towards the end of the school year, I started to panic. School would be ending for summer break and so would my job. God came through again. I found a job at McDonald's. Initially, McDonald's gave me 25-30 hours per week to work. I had no time at all for silliness and getting into trouble.

In all, I lived with my god-sister 8-10 months. Due to the pressures of her being a new mom and the strain of trying to find her own way, my mother said that I should move back home. I promptly refused.

I was reluctant at first but decided that it would be impossible to rent and maintain my own place at 16 years old. Being out of the house for that short period of time taught me the importance of positive and constructive activities to fill my time with.

Not only in my own situation but also observing other families. If a family has alternate activities for their kids, their children were less likely to fall into trouble.

The key to keeping your youngsters out of trouble is to keep them busy. It doesn't matter if you have sons or daughters, keeping them busy with *constructive* activities makes a parent's job so much easier.

Currently, in America, some parents have done a good job using the popularity of sports as an avenue to better their children and align them with the benefits that sports participation has to offer.

I caution you not to be one-sided when helping your child choose activities that they may want to participate in. Whether your child participates in sports, reading lab, math lab, entrepreneur club, or Saturday school the goal here is to keep their minds occupied.

An idle mind is the devil's Playground
- Proverbs 4,8

Don't get me wrong, sports participation is great. But more diverse activities chosen for participation can and will make your child more well-rounded. Expose your child to a variety of activities such as math competitions, young entrepreneur seminars, Junior Achievement, youth engineering competitions, robot battles, etc. Your child also having so-called "basketball cred" can't hurt, but having success in academic competitions as well will go a long way toward your child's long-term prosperity. Our children have to know that "A.I." can mean Artificial Intelligence as well as Allen Iverson.

5. Be Nosey and Try to Understand Your Child

Really get to know your child. Don't just think that you know your children. Pay attention to your child's social media footprint and cell phone usage. To keep your children safe don't be opposed to loading cell phone monitoring software to actually see what your kids are doing and with whom.

You might not like the idea of seemingly being overly curious or facing the possibility of spying on your children, but children may be unwilling or unable to ask for help when they need it. While you may have to play the bad guy on occasion, keeping your kids safe is the priority. On occasion, you may need to act like a stealth detective in order to find out what your kids are up too. This seems to be especially true for preteens and teenagers.

Teenagers are not smaller adults! They are bigger children. Even when you think you are aware of what is going on, stop and look even harder. When my daughter was approximately 14 years old, she drank rubbing alcohol trying to escape reality. Later I found out that she also had been contemplating suicide. All this over teen social issues. My wife was really on top of it when it came to really watching my daughter. She found my daughter sitting on the floor in her room and not being very responsive to various questions. Later after a very large emergency room bill, we find out what happened. Up until that point I had chided my wife on several occasions to give our teen daughter more privacy. *I was wrong*! I learned my lesson. During my son's teen years, I watched him like a hawk. Of course, I tried to be as unobtrusive as possible.

Yes, you do have to give your teens a little independence. You need to give them what I call "supervised independence". What I mean by this is independence with constant follow-up and investigation.

This will be a balancing act. As parents, you *must* find out what your kids are doing or planning to do. But it has to be done in a way that your teen doesn't feel that you are being intrusive. If your teens and or pre-teens feel that you are being overly intrusive, they may shut down. If they attempt to shut you out, it will be way harder to figure out what is going on.

The best technique I've found is an investigation through casual conversation, *without* an accusatory tone. Start having these stress-free conversations with your children while they are at preschool age if possible. My mother would start my sisters and I talking about anything and nothing in particular. Before we knew it, we'd divulged every bit of information about our entire day. The key here was the non-threatening tone of the conversation.

If your child is a teen and you are just now opening the lines of communication, ***please start slow***. I know how this is going to sound, but you have to earn their trust all over again. If possible, find a topic of common interest to both you and your teen and start the conversation there.

If there is no common topic. Try to genuinely show interest in something that your child is interested in. The tone of these conversations should be low-key and non-threatening to your teen. The idea is to get your child comfortable talking to you.

When talking with your child try to have them do most of the talking. You just listen and maybe bob your head every once in a while. *Fight the urge to interject.* These are not teaching or preaching moments. These are listening moments!

One of the best weapons to use in order to find out information about your child is at the dinner table. Yes, the dinner table. Growing up we only ate together on Sundays. And then it was usually around the television. Not so with my then future wife's family. They ate together almost every meal, and they actually talked around the dinner table.

My wife and I started dating around the age of 16 - 17. My future in-laws invited me to dinner quite often. I loved my mother-in-law's cooking so it was a win-win as far as I was concerned.

My father-in-law would start the conversation off with something non-threatening such as baseball (I loved baseball at the time). He would start me talking and before I knew it, I was talking about his daughter and telling him all about myself. He was a master at getting information on us kids.

Later when we had our own children, we used a similar technique. This worked really well with my son. My wife would cook my son's favorite meal and over dinner, we would casually steer the conversation to whatever we were trying to find out. Sometimes we would ask the kids how their friends were handling a certain situation. This was an easy non-threatening way to further investigate concerns that we may have had about our kids. These casual conversations allowed us to really see what was happening in the lives of our children.

Also, understand that kids are naturals when it comes to counter espionage. During these conversations, they may throw out something just to get a rise out of you or to just test your reaction. Stay calm. Don't fall for the bait. Don't forget that no matter how smart your child is, you have real-world experience.

I learned quite a bit from my father-in-law in these situations such as to his ability to stay calm when a conversation went a little sideways. Be ready. When or and if your child opens up, you'll hear things that may cause your hair to stand on edge, make you want to scream to the top of your lungs, and or want to choke your teenager like a chicken. Don't do any of it! Remember these are not teaching or preaching moments, but listening moments. Also, remind yourself that *you do love these children*!

When you find yourself in this situation borrow my father-in-law's wit. He would chuckle and then say, "I have faith in you, and I know that you will make the right decision.". After these conversations, I usually did make the right decision, because I didn't want to let my then future father-in-law down. Years later after my wife and I had gotten married she would tease me saying, "You just married me to get into my father's family.". I don't believe that that was the case, but my father-in-law was a huge blessing to me over the 22 years I had with him before his passing.

My in-laws had their children later in life. My father-in-law was even older than my grandfather. As such he had tons of life experiences. We often talked about child-rearing even before I actually had children. Thinking back on it now, that seemed odd. Maybe he was priming me for parenthood. Nevertheless, my children benefited immensely from his experiences and the conversations he and I had over the years.

During our conversations, he explained things that he did wrong and things that he did right with his own child-rearing. His biggest regret was not keeping a closer eye on Larry, my wife's youngest brother. He said that he trusted him too much and really didn't see what was going on until it was too late. He warned me that no matter what I had going on that the kids had to come first.

I had fallen into the trap of being busy trying to make a better life for the kids and not being there for the kids. This was during my daughter's early teen years. During this time, I worked a full-time job, ran a dojo, attended college part-time, and tried to start a 2nd business all at the same time. Something had to give. I put the brakes on. My father-in-law was right. My kids just wanted me. I am sure that your kids just want to spend time with you too.

The secret to understanding your children is no secret at all. Just talk to your kids and spend quality time with them. As parents, it is easy to fall into the trap of earning a living and putting our kids on the back burner.

Yes, during certain periods of time, you may be required to be away from your children more than you would like. Especially due to career restraints. Talk to your kids and explain to them what the end goal is. Promise them some makeup time, and **keep** that promise. Remember your kids love you more than any amount of junk that you could buy them.

Understanding your child is one of the most important things that you should learn as a parent. It is very helpful in becoming effective in guiding and nurturing your child as they grow and mature. You need to bear in mind that your child has a unique personality trait that remains consistent throughout life.

One of the ways you can understand your child is by observing them as they sleep, eat, or play. Look for the consistent traits. Which activities do they like best? Is adjusting to changes easy for them or do they need time to become familiar with these things?

These things are the normal characteristics of a child and your child may not be an exception. As much as possible, have time to talk to your children as this is crucial to gaining information and understanding. In the case of young children, they require less verbal language and more facial expression and body language in order to understand their thoughts and feelings. Asking them questions will allow them to share their feelings to you.

For example, rather than asking them what they did in school, ask them what they built with their blocks today. Instead of asking them if they played with their playmate, focus on the game they played.

- By Robert Myers, Ph.D. - Child Psychologist
Excerpted from Child Development Institute

For some parents, teenagers present our greatest challenge to parenthood. Oftentimes teenagers can seem unreasonable, moody, and hard to get along with. The crazy thing is they are thinking the same thing about us. Try and keep the lines of communication open and really pay attention to what your kids do and say. Don't trust them too much to their own designs. Be involved. Even if you are frustrated, don't throw your hand s into the air and give up. The teen and pre-teen years are just a phase. You will survive these years, and with your help so will your children.

6. Spiritual Foundation

"The human spirit is stronger than anything that can happen to it."

- George C. Scott

The above quote is quite true. I'll add one thing though - the spirit is stronger if it has been refined or cultivated. In order for our children to progress to maturity and become successful adults, it is imperative that they develop a sense of resiliency against life's many hurdles. A true spiritual foundation can offer that resiliency.

"Within the covers of the Bible are the answers for all the problems men face"

- Ronald Reagan 40th U.S. President

Throughout human history, spiritual foundations and strong inner belief systems have given men the willpower and hope necessary to overcome even the most troubling of times. As such when we give our children a strong spiritual foundation, they are then equipped to handle the hurdles of life.

"My call to the ministry was not a miraculous or supernatural something...On the contrary, it was an inner urge calling me to serve humanity."
- Dr. Martin Luther King Jr.

At its most basic level, a strong spiritual foundation places the right mental attitude at the core of our being. The problems facing Black America and America as a whole is a problem of diminutive moral attitudes in general and specifically spiritual decrepitude.

"Life is 10% what happens to you and 90% how we react to it"
- Charles R. Swindoll

The above quote by Charles R. Swindoll has proven true in my own personal experiences and outlook on life's setbacks. Please ingrain it into your heart and the heart of your children.

In America today we seem to have acquiesced to an attitude of victimization and finger-pointing instead of being defiant in the face of adversity. This is what therapist Izzy Kalman wrote on the subject for an article posted on Mar 16, 2018, on Phycology Today's website:

It (political correctness) has instilled in our population a victim mentality that absolves us from personal responsibility for our difficult life situations and instructs us instead to blame others and to demand that our government protect us from all unpleasant experiences. Rather than advancing harmony and understanding, as intended, political correctness has fostered hatred and violence, as people blame each other for their misery and groups fight each other for superior claims to victimhood.

We must teach our children to stand up and take charge of their lives. Teach them to learn something from life's ups and downs, then move on! In order for America to survive and thrive, we must renew the "can do" spirit of our country along with strengthening the moral fortitude of our society.

The idea that "anything goes" is not freedom. In actuality, this is an affront to true freedom. Remember, America's freedoms *can't* be bought or sold. They must be won, over and over again. Common decency must be the starting point!

The attitudes of ethical decay are symptomatic of the political morass and partisan infighting on display every day by our elected officials in government. Common sense ethics and dignity must once again be placed at the forefront of the American psyche.

"The fundamental basis of this nation's law was given to Moses on the Mount. The fundamental basis of our Bill of Rights comes from the teaching we get from Exodus and St. Mathew, from Isaiah and St. Paul. I don't think we emphasize that enough these days. If we don't have the proper fundamental moral background, we will finally end up with a totalitarian government which does not believe in the right for anybody except the state."

\- Harry S. Truman 33rd U.S. President

It doesn't matter what your religious preferences are. All the major religions stress basic human ethics and attempt to give you a foundation of spiritual strength. For generations of African Americans, this foundation has been the Black Church and it has been accessed and leaned on in times of crisis and need.

By the 1790s, as more and more migrants fled southern states and settled in northern cities, some white evangelical leaders sought to control black members by seating them separately and by strengthening white control over the churches.

At the same time black leaders such as Richard Allen and Absalom Jones, many of whom were educated, literate, and ready to organize, began to desire their own independent black churches. In cities with large numbers of freed blacks such as Philadelphia, Boston, and New York, leaders broke away from white Methodists and Baptists. By 1816, the first independent black denomination, the African Methodist Episcopal Church, came into existence and was quickly followed by the African Methodist Episcopal Zion Church in 1821.

In these independent churches, African Americans combined evangelical zeal with work on behalf of struggling free blacks and antislavery advocacy. Because limited educational and vocational opportunities were open to blacks in northern states, churches also served as schools, training centers, and centers of community organization. Many of the early black newspapers published were facilitated or spearheaded by black clergy, and thus the churches helped to bring African Americans across distances together into a more self-conscious community.

Laurie Maffly-Kipp
African American Christianity, Pt. I, To the Civil War
University of North Carolina at Chapel Hill
©National Humanities Center

As you can see from the excerpt printed above, African Americans have a long history of interaction with and receiving help from the Black Church. I'm not trying to preach religion, or even tell you religion is necessary. I will tell you that my faith in God has sustained me and my family through the many trials that life has thrust on us. When you are going through something, it is a good feeling to know that you are not alone. My belief system has given me something to lean on. Several times throughout my life this faith has had to prop me up when nothing else would.

I know that the current headlines list all types of misdeeds of priests and pastors worldwide. You yourself may have been mistreated at a church, synagogue, or temple. Keep in mind that organized religion is run by people.

Since no person is even remotely perfect, it is impossible for these organizations to be perfect either. When I speak about religion, I'm speaking about establishing a *personal relationship* with whatever God you believe in. This internal relationship focus can and will help empower both you and your child.

My people are destroyed from lack of knowledge. Because you have rejected knowledge, I also reject you as my priests; because you have ignored the law of your God, I also will ignore your children.

\- Hosea 4,6

In Western Society, all of our basic laws stem from the Bible. In the Middle East, those countries' basic laws stem from the Koran. In Asia, all basic laws stem from Confucianism and or Buddhism. As such we have to at least start the moral and ethical conversation by acknowledging the importance of a religious slant.

I know that in America right now, religion is not considered cool. This is especially true with our nation's youth and young adults. Over the years I've personally observed very interesting phenomena among many so-called atheists. When confronted by catastrophic life events, *every time* they shouted "Oh God!" Food for thought.

It won't hurt to expose your children to the great moralistic stories and examples found in religious teachings. Also, it can't hurt to give your child something that they can hold onto that is bigger than themselves. In times of need, we all may need something to grab ahold of to sustain us. If nothing else, expose your children to the many inspirational heroes depicted in the various religious texts. As a child, I loved those stories, as did my own children.

Whether you follow the Bible, Koran, Torah, Tao, Buddhist scriptures, or whatever text you believe, all of the major religions can be distilled down to treating your fellow man with love and respect. They also attempt to instill a positive can-do attitude towards life.

The choice is yours. You can try to give your child a strong spiritual foundation or let them keep being influenced by the carnal, sordid input from mass media and the world at large.

When our children miss the mark when it comes to decency and ethical behavior they are being set up for the consequences of life. These consequences will lead to their downfall and destruction.

By teaching your child to have respect, decency, and correct moral behavior towards others - they should and will, in turn, be respected.

Train up a child in the way he should go;
Even when he is old, he will not depart from it.
- Proverbs 22,6

---

7. Encourage Your Child to Read

"Once you learn to read, you will be forever free."

\- Frederick Douglass

Education is another cornerstone of success here in America. We are now living in the information age. If your child can't or won't read, his or her growth will be impeded. They will be unable to access or even pick through the deluge of information being thrown at us daily.

"There is nothing which can better deserve our patronage than the promotion of science and literature. Knowledge is in every country the surest basis of public happiness."

\- George Washington

Going forward in America education will be a requirement of success. My father-in-law came of age in the 1930s. He told me that the labor market at that time was based on physical labor. He said "the bigger and stronger you looked the better job you could get, but going forward jobs will be based on how much you know.". We had that conversation in 1987. In today's society, that statement is truer than ever.

> *"Some know the value of education by having it. I knew its value by not having it."*
>
> - Frederick Douglass

There can be _No Compromise_ when it comes to reading. My maternal Grandfather didn't finish the 3rd grade, but he demanded that we do well in school. My Grandfather spoiled me and would let me do whatever I wanted to do, except when it came to school.

When it came to education, he demanded success. He only disciplined or scolded me twice in my whole life! Once when I was 8 and again at 15. Both times it centered around school or reading.

My Grandfather told me the story of how he and his brother were forced to leave school in the 3rd and 2nd grade respectively. Their family was sharecropping in Arkansas and the farmer who owned the land brought their father to the schoolhouse and demanded that "you take them boys out of here, school don't do nothin but spoil a n___r".

My Grandfather said that he loved school and was angry his whole life about that situation. He used to say, "boy if you get an education you can be anything that you want to be, but if you don't, I'm gonna hit you so hard I'm gonna turn your nose up and let it rain in it!". I didn't know exactly what that meant and I didn't want to find out!

Blessed are those who find wisdom,
those who gain understanding,
for she is more profitable than silver
and yields better returns than gold.
- Proverbs 3,13-14

Having our kids read will open up American and African American history. Which in turn gives our children both national and ethnic pride.

Studying history is important because it allows us to
understand our past, which in turn allows us to
understand our present.
If we want to know how and why our world is the way it
is today, we have to look to history for answers.
- *WWW.ENOTES.COM*

Without reading - this understanding of who we are as a people or how we came to be as a country is impossible to grasp. And grasp it we must in order to move the country and ourselves forward. Make no mistake our shared history, folklore, and stories still shape us today.

African Americans' folklore allowed them to hold on to their roots, their identity, and their hope for the future.

In today's world, these ancient stories and traditions continue to offer strength and dignity.

- Excerpt from Ethnic Folklore by Ellyn Sann

I started out in school as a poor reader. I remember getting grades of "N - Needs Improvement" in the 1st and 2nd grades. My parents and grandparents were proactive when it came to reading. My Maternal Grandmother (Miss Ann) started going to night school so she could help me. As a child, she was forced to quit school in the 1st- grade to help care for an elderly relative and never learned to read as a child. I remember that she used to mark things with an "X" as her signature. In a little over a year, she got her reading comprehension to 3rd-grade level. I remember how proud she was to be able to read the daily newspaper. Once she was able to read at that level, she wouldn't accept any lack of effort on my end. Even though she whipped my butt for everything else, she never spanked me about reading. I can still hear her saying "just hang in there you'll get it" as she patted me on the head or shoulder.

Thanks, Ms. Ann, for always believing in me!

My mother used to make me sit down with her and drill on phonics and then drill some more. Boy, I hated reading. When it came to reading, there was nothing but punishments and scolding from my mother. I thought that I would never get the hang of reading.

Thank God for my Stepfather. With his help, I had a total paradigm shift. He taught me to love to read. We would *play* reading games in the car whenever we went anywhere together! He would have me read street signs, names on buildings, license plates, anything! He then bought me comic books to read. He told my mom that it didn't matter what I read as long as I was reading something. My dad and grandmother made friends with Mr. David, a geeky older neighbor who collected comics. He owned hundreds of comics. I would go over there and read even more. Grandma and Grandpa Watts bought me books for birthdays and Christmas gifts. After a while, I couldn't stop reading.

After all this reading a funny thing happened. In the 7th grade, I took one of the State's Standardized Tests and scored at a reading level of 12th grade. This shocked my teachers and the whole family. I never looked back.

Since my younger siblings saw me constantly reading and there were so many books in the house, they just naturally gravitated to reading at high levels. I remember them being able to read my old 3rd and 4th-grade readers while they were in kindergarten or 1st grade. Reading is truly contagious. Even today I ask for books as gifts.

The large majority of highly successful people are avid readers. Whether it is self-help books, trade journals, sales primers, history books, the Holy Bible, the Holy Koran, the Torah, the I-Ching, biographies, etc. You get the drift; it doesn't matter what our kids read as long as they read.

A word of caution. When it comes to reading; spanking, scolding, punishments, etc. don't work long term. The idea here is to get your children to love to read. It will open up a world of possibilities if you can figure out how to make it fun and interesting for *your* child.

My Dad figured it out. If a child is interested in a particular subject, they will want to learn more about it. Make use of all the tools at your disposal such as flashcards, songs, board games, computer games, the library, book clubs, etc.

Let your kids see you read. My mom read mostly romance novels, while dad read sci-fi, historical dramas, and military history.

When my siblings were younger, whenever my mom would need a sanity break, she would say "turn off the television and the radio, everybody get a book". The house would be quiet at least for a while until the girls would complain "I've read these books ten times or more". My mom would chime in and say "read them again".

By all means, start early. Read to your children when they are babies and toddlers. In today's competitive environment your child should have the rudiments of reading down pat by age 3 - 4. Start when your child is about 1-2 years old teaching them the alphabet and numbers 1-10. Again, make it seem like playing and your kids will get it without being stressed out and most importantly without stressing you out.

Don't let your kids start school already behind! But if your child is already behind - the good news is that they can catch up rather quickly. Kids are sponges. They can pick up anything they want too. Think about the songs on the radio that they know all the words too, or the electronic devices that they can master in just a few minutes. Your kids can do it!

There are tons of studies out there tying the increasing incarceration rates of black youth to the lack of a good education and or poor reading skills. Developing strong reading skills seems to be even more important for our male children.

Black boys are not reading at an adequate level.

> *In 2014, the Black Star Project published findings that just 10 percent of eighth-grade Black boys in the U.S. are considered "proficient" in reading. In urban areas like Chicago and Detroit, that number was even lower. By contrast, the 2013 National Assessment of Education Progress found that 46 percent of white students are adequate readers by eighth grade, and 17 percent of Black students as a whole are too. The achievement gap between the two races is startling,*

but the difference between the NAEP report on Black students as a whole and the Black Star findings of just Black boys is troubling too. It is not simply Black children in general who appear to be failing in the basics – like literacy; it is the boys.

- Dr. Matthew Lynch excerpted from Education Week

Interestingly enough we are sending a disproportionate number of young African-American men to prison instead of educating them. According to the Federal Bureau of Prisons, as of November 2018, 38.1% of the current prison population is Black men. A 2014 USA Today article states that more than 40% of Black men will be arrested by the age of 23. Per the Schott Foundation for Public Education, only 59% of African-Americans are graduating from high school, and only 47% are graduating on time. These numbers **cannot** be good for America.

The educational challenges facing the African-American segment of our population has less to do with race but is more a problem of class. Poorer underachieving schools seemed to always be found in poorer communities. If we want to turn our neighborhoods around, we must first turn our schools around.

Let's talk about education in general. We expect our leaders to be educated. We all hope our children will grow into leaders. As such we should also expect and demand that they become educated. By educated I don't necessarily mean earning a college degree. There have been countless examples of successful people not earning a college degree. The most famous are Bill Gates, the co-founder of Microsoft Corporation, and Steve Jobs, the co-founder of Apple Computer.

If college is what your child wants and needs to do, by all means, help them make it happen. But, don't send them to college just in hopes of securing the next hot job without having a plan to ensure graduation. Please understand that for the majority of college students if they don't graduate, they have just wasted time and accrued massive debt! Have a *Graduation* plan, and work the plan!

Again, if college is in your child's future let's make sure that they have the tools to succeed and *graduate*. Parents at the end of the day "We" are responsible for our children's academic preparation or lack thereof. If you have a 9th or 10th grader that has a 5th-grade reading level and you are hoping for your child's success in life, you'd better get involved quickly and be proactive.

Make selective use of the resources that you do have. When my son was a teenager the average cost for a video game was approximately $59 and tutoring sessions were only $20 per hour. Extra help workbooks were priced around $30. Nowadays YouTube how-to videos are free. If your kids need extra help *find it*!

Start by having family meetings to discuss how college is to be funded. Come up with a realistic plan to pay for college, and understand the real cost of higher education.

Don't set your kids up for failure. So many able-bodied African American students are enrolled in institutions of higher learning but don't graduate. According to "The Journal of Blacks in Higher Education" only 42% of black college students graduate with a degree. Even though our inner-city K-12 schools seem to consistently drop the ball when it comes to college preparedness. Black students overwhelmingly overcome this obstacle and can do well in college. The biggest obstacle to black graduation rates seems to be the financial constraints. The journal listed above quotes a report from Nellie Mae (the largest nonprofit provider of federal and private student loans in the country) states "69% of African Americans who enrolled in college but did finish said that they left college because of high student loan debt".

Make no mistake when it comes to college, graduation is the goal. Not just getting accepted and attending. Stop setting our kids up for failure. For example, after reviewing the educational cost of your child's college of choice. If the financial plan of grants, scholarships, work-study, and loans, etc. still shows a deficit of $20,000 per school year. You and your family should look at other options. That $20,000 deficit is not just going away. Maybe you can look at a less expensive school,

Community College, online classes, etc. Unless you have a rich uncle, who can pay the balance, your child won't be able to graduate.

Even worse if your child does attend this school and is unable to graduate, now they will have student loan debt that can and will destroy your child's credit score even before they can get started in life. They won't be able to transfer any credits earned to another school because they'll still owe money to that school. Your child will now be stuck. No education, bad credit, and tens of thousands of dollars in debt that their minimum wage salary can't support.

If college is on your family's horizon do all that you can to ensure success for your child. It's ok to be proud that your child is accepted and will attend a college or university of their choice. Trust me, you will be even prouder when they graduate.

College can and should be a huge eye-opener and paradigm shift. Encourage them to go to college for the experience and the education. College forces you to interact with different cultures and ideas that you probably wouldn't normally be exposed to. College can also be fun for most young people.

Even if your child doesn't want to go to college, reading skill is still the prerequisite of success. All high-income fields that don't require a college education such as business ownership, plumbing, electrical, computer network support, loan officer, automotive technicians, web developer and coder, air traffic controllers, etc., have a few things in common. One, no college degree required. Two, extensive training (i.e.-reading) is needed.

In the current computer age, just about every career imaginable requires some level of reading comprehension. The National Institute of Child Health and Human Development says, "Reading is the single most important skill necessary for a happy, productive and successful life."

Reading is such a powerful tool.

8. Don't SPOIL Your Children, It's Okay to Say NO!

"It is easier to build strong children than to repair broken men."

- Frederick Douglass

If you want to be able to enjoy your middle years and beyond, you better teach your children to be independent. I've observed a troubling phenomenon in modern families. It seems that some kids can't or won't grow up!

I want to be very clear here. I'm not speaking about children or grandchildren who have had to come back home for a while due to the economic realities of the times that we live in. I'm speaking specifically to the situations of children not launching to adulthood. I've personally witnessed families that have grown children living at their parents' home with their own children for *years*, all mooching off of good old mom and dad. Once your children are adults, your only responsibility to them is to try and maintain family ties with them.

It's not your job to financially support your children until you are dead! Unless your child is a special needs child; you are not obligated to pay their rent, buy groceries, buy clothes, repair automobiles, or provide unlimited babysitting and child-rearing services *indefinitely*. Look what a well-known doctor has to say on the subject.

A spoiled child may be recognized by an unwillingness to conform to the ordinary demand s of living in a family, for example, a refusal to come for dinner on time, a demand for attention or for a privilege denied to others, a strategy for getting his or her way by creating a fuss publicly.

The spoiled child is likely to be irritable and unsympathetic to others. He seems comfortable ignoring his parents' wishes. "He wants what he wants when he wants it." For that reason, he may seem to be impulsive. The spoiled child is likely to grow up to be a spoiled adult.

The problem with being a "spoiled adult" goes far beyond the fact that such an individual, demanding much of the time, is likely to seem unpleasant, even obnoxious, to the people around him. A spoiled person is unhappy. He feels frustrated, even cheated, if he or she is not allowed to indulge his or her wishes immediately. Being spoiled suggests to most people a desire for more and more possessions, and that is indeed one aspect of being spoiled, but another is an unwillingness to conform to ordinary social expectations. Somebody who won't do what he or she is expected to do is spoiled. That person may seem disgruntled, complaining, resentful, and self-centered. Such a person is preoccupied by thoughts of what he or she does not have. And lacking discipline, that person may fail at work and in social situations.

Fredric Neuman M.D.

Excerpted from Psychology Today

At some point in life, everyone may need some type of help at least once. I'm not saying don't help out your adult children or grandchildren. But your children and grandchildren have to know that any support given is *finite*.

This chapter is a sensitive subject for me. Over the years my mother has given much more financial help and gifts to my sisters than myself. I didn't like it, but I understood it from her perspective on the necessity of men being strong and self-sufficient.

My mother told me that one of the reasons that she was so hard on me growing up was because she was afraid that I'd grow into adulthood unprepared, unable to take care of myself. Growing up, we had an adult family member who didn't seem able to take care of himself even though he had a full-time job. He constantly approached my mother for financial support. If you have adult children that are constantly seeking financial support it may be past time for a firmer stance on adult responsibility. Use this opportunity as a teaching moment for your adult child or adult grandchild.

Sometimes you must simply express your understanding of their plight and only offer suggestions on how *they* can address the situation. You do more damage than good to your adult children and adult grandchildren by *constantly* jumping in with the checkbook or debit card to save the day.

Remember you can only do so much to help your adult children. Hardly anyone has unlimited financial resources, and you won't always be there to help them. Since this is the case, teach your kids how to be independent and demand it! Per my Mom, it is critical for male children to grow up with an understanding of responsibility. American culture generally accepts that boys will grow up and assume roles as head of household, provider, and protector of the family unit.

If your adult son or adult grandson can't or won't take responsibility for themselves and or their families, this is a huge problem. I want to remind you again that most of us don't have unlimited resources, so don't act like it. The reality is that you can't support and spoil your grown son or grown grandson indefinitely. Place limits and boundaries on any help given.

Historically during slavery, the black man could not assume the role of family protector and or provider. Black women could say and do things that would have gotten the black man killed just for saying or doing the exact same things. During these times it was dangerous for black men in general. As a black man or black youth, you could be killed for any minor infraction or perceived act of disrespect. As such black women were forced into roles of family leadership while black men were largely marginalized.

We can't change history, but we can take charge and redirect our future. Let's teach our sons how to take their place as role models, providers, and protectors of the family. Once this happens on a large scale, we change the direction of Black America to a more positive trend. This positive trend will also positively affect America as a whole.

Let's not let our daughters off the hook either. The new marginalizing force in Black America and America as a whole is a combination of incarceration, lack of education, and abject poverty. In this environment, black women have to be stronger than ever. Black women have disproportionally endured the hardships and aftermath of single-parent households, generational family poverty, loneliness, low wages, and poor health care. For the success and strengthening of black families, women will have to be at the forefront in demanding their just due.

Black America *can't* accept the raising of mediocre children. Parents, let's stop marginalizing our children by spoiling them to the point that they are unable to take their rightful place in America.

Okay, Black Families we know how we got here, now what are we going to do about it? Remember Institutional Slavery is dead!

9. Don't Be Afraid to Discipline Your Children

As children, I'm sure some of us vowed to ourselves that when we grew up and had children that we wouldn't discipline them the same way our parents did. I remember telling myself that I'm going to let my kids do whatever they wanted to do. Of course, for my children's safety and my own sanity, this was not possible.

Your child's formative years are the best times to institute your rules and establish guidelines for acceptable behavior. Hopefully, as your child matures any needed discipline will be replaced by your child's ever-expanding self-discipline.

"Self-discipline is the ability to do what you should do when you should do it, whether you want to or not."

- Dennis Kimbro and Napoleon Hill

Think and Grow Rich - A Black Choice

Discipline seems to be about staying plugged into our children's lives. Over the years I noticed that when I was totally immersed in my children's lives, discipline was much easier. During these times discipline became just minor correcting. It seemed to be much more of a teaching session than a full-blown stressful disciplinary situation.

I want to make something very clear here. Staying plugged into our adolescent and teenage children's lives should *not* be considered prying nor intruding! And if it is, so what? Our children can get into trouble if left to their own devices. If you value your children's safety you will discipline them.

From a scientific standpoint, our children's brains are underdeveloped until adulthood. Look at the following report from the University of Rochester Medical Center's Health Encyclopedia,

Understanding the Teen Brain

It doesn't matter how smart teens are or how well they scored on the SAT or ACT. Good judgment isn't something they can excel in, at least not yet.

The rational part of a teen's brain isn't fully developed and won't be until age 25 or so.

In fact, recent research has found that adult and teen brains work differently. Adults think with the prefrontal cortex, the brain's rational part. This is the part of the brain that responds to situations with good judgment and an awareness of long-term consequences. Teens process information with the amygdala. This is the emotional part.

In teen's brains, the connections between the emotional part of the brain and the decision-making center are still developing—and not necessarily at the same rate. That's why when teens experience overwhelming emotional input, they can't explain later what they were thinking. They weren't thinking as much as they were feeling.

What's a parent to do?

You're the most important role model your kids have. Sure, their friends are important to them, but the way you behave and fulfill your responsibilities will have a profound and long-lasting effect on your children.

- *Discussing the consequences of their actions can help teens link impulsive thinking with facts. This helps the brain make these connections and wires the brain to make this link more often.*

- *Remind your teens that they're resilient and competent. Because they're so focused on the moment, adolescents have trouble seeing they can play a part in changing bad situations. It can help to remind them of times in the past they thought would be devastating but turned out for the best.*

- *Become familiar with things that are important to your teens. It doesn't mean you have to like hip-hop music, but showing an interest in the things they're involved in shows them they're important to you.*

- *Ask teens if they want you to respond when they come to you with problems, or if they just want you to listen.*

Parents tend to jump in with advice to try to fix their children's problems or place blame. But this can make teens less likely to be open with their parents in the future. You want to make it emotionally safe and easy for them to come to you, so you can be part of their lives.

Signs of trouble

It's normal for teens to be down or out of sorts for a couple of days. But if you see a significant mood or behavioral change that lasts more than 2 weeks, it could mean something else is going on, such as depression.

If you think your teen could be depressed, promptly seek professional treatment for your child. Depression is serious and, if left untreated, can be life-threatening.

Your teen needs your guidance, even though they may think they don't. Understanding their development can help you support them in becoming independent, responsible adults.

I want to mention three families from my youth that seemed to be very successful in raising their children by staying plugged in. They were the Gardner's, Teasley's, and the Stansberry's. These parents seemed to be everywhere all the time. Mrs. Gardner and Mrs. Stansberry volunteered and worked at our elementary school. Mrs. Teasley was always dropping in at the school talking to teachers. I can still see Mr. Garner walking around in his work clothes constantly checking in on the neighborhood kids. I still remember that big smile and him, asking, "What you boys doing?"

On occasion, the neighborhood kids would be corrected by Mr. and Mrs. Gardner or Mrs. Stansberry, but it didn't feel like discipline. Kids in the neighborhood understood that these folks loved us and were looking out for us, so we tried to be on our best behavior around them or anywhere close to their homes.

Listen to advice and accept discipline, and at the end, you will be counted among the wise.

\- Proverbs 19,20

I'm not looking back through rose-colored glasses either. We also knew that Mr. and Mrs. Gardner and Mrs. Stansberry would whip your butt if need be. Especially, Mrs. Stansberry, she was a no-nonsense parent who expected the best out of you - no excuses!

As a child, I often heard Ms. Ann (maternal grandmother) talking with her friends saying - "Child if you don't discipline them kids the police will". The police nor the authorities are always right, but we must still teach our kids to respect authority. This starts with your authority.

Without the police, society would turn to anarchy and chaos very quickly. Because of what's going on in the news right now I believe that I must speak about our children's interaction with the police.

My wife called it the police talk. I tried passing on to son what was taught to me concerning the police. My grandmother taught me to always be respectful of the police, and not to try anything crazy when confronted by the police. Her logic was that 98% of the police are good people just trying to serve the community.

The other 2% are just troublemakers looking to act tough and to exert their authority on you. She went on to say that if and when you are confronted by the police, don't resist or attempt to fight and flee. Don't give the bad 2% of police any reason to hurt you.

Also, if you are not resisting and you're still injured during an arrest, you have legal recourse. You don't have any recourse if you are dead!

Yes, it is not fair that we have to have a special talk or training for our sons or daughters on how to deal with the police. But unfortunately, this is where we find ourselves in 21st century America. As we keep striving to move forward and upward to our rightful place as leaders, role models, and possessors of a true place in America, this civic atrocity will melt away into history. Then, America will be better for it.

As a child, I hated to be told anything, but as an adult, I appreciate most of the discipline I received as a child.

Discipline your children, and they will give you peace; they will bring you the delights you desire.

- Proverbs 29,17

Again, teach your kids to respect authority. Also, teach them to hold authority accountable, and stay plugged into what is going on. I don't agree with all the politics of Al Sharpton, but I respect his methods of holding the authorities accountable. If and when he feels that there is an injustice, he uses *all* the legal means at his disposal to take action. Whether protest rallies, get out the vote campaigns, petition drives, meetings with civic and government leaders, etc. He's plugged in.

Teaching your kids to respect authority starts with them learning to respect your authority and your home. Don't be afraid to discipline your children. The method that you use must be comfortable for you. Whether you believe in spankings, punishments or time-outs, etc. it doesn't matter as long as you are *consistent* and as fair as possible.

My son, do not despise the Lord's discipline,
and do not resent his rebuke,
because the Lord disciplines those he loves,
as a father, the son he delights in.

- Proverbs 3,11-12

I can't tell you how you should discipline your children, but I caution you on spanking *excessively*. In my opinion, spanking should be a last resort. My maternal grandmother believed in spanking for any infraction no matter how minor. During a short period of my life, I probably received two spankings a day every day. Yeah, I probably earned most of them. She would spank me with belts, ironing cords, switches, anything that she could grab. One time my legs were bruised and bloody from getting spanked with switches. It was so bad that when my grandfather came back home, my grandparents got into a big fight over it.

Looking back, it may have bordered on abuse. But the reality was excessive spanking didn't work. It only made me tough and gave me a high pain tolerance. After a while, I didn't even mind the spankings anymore, because I knew that when it was over, I was going to go right back to doing what I wanted to do.

Yes, I understand that sometimes spanking is necessary, and yes, I did spank my children on occasion. But, for me and then for my children punishments seemed to work best. I hated punishments as a child so I was mostly on good behavior when around my mother who really believed in putting you on punishment. Her punishment was to take away the things you liked the most.

As I remember it her discipline methods were more of a stair step. First came the discussions and teaching moments on why not to do a certain thing. Then if you persisted then came the stern scolding's. If you still wouldn't conform to the house rules, she would then break out the punishments. If she had to break out the spankings this meant that you usually would have had to do something crazy or potentially harmful.

Growing up I saw my mother mostly on weekends and during the summer and winter breaks until moving in with her full time at age 14. My mother nor her mother were very emotionally nurturing, but my mother tried hard to be fair. She would take the time and try to explain why you had to do something a certain way. Then if you continued to act out then the reprimands and punishments came.

She would hold you accountable for the full term of the punishment. You served the whole punishment no matter if it was one week, two weeks, or two months. Once I was put on punishment for five months for stealing. I thought that I was going to lose my mind, but it worked. I never stole *anything* again. This incident happened when I was 13 years old. I was out shoveling snow with my friends trying to earn some extra pocket money and I didn't have any work gloves. After earning some money, we went to the neighborhood market to buy treats. While there I decided I would buy some work gloves because they were only a dollar.

One of my so-called friends chimed in; "Man don't pay for those, just put them in your pocket. You can use that dollar to buy some more chips and candy." At first, I declined. They kept goading me, calling me scared. Like any self-respecting 13-year-old out to prove their manhood, I folded to peer pressure. I was promptly caught and ordered to go home and get my mother and to bring her back up to the store. After going home and explaining the situation to my mother she became furious. I thought that her eyes were going to pop out of her head from anger. She marched me back to the store giving me the most severe verbal lashing she could. Once at the store she apologized profusely to Ms. Laura (proprietor) retrieved the gloves that I had tried to steal and made me pay for them.

I was so embarrassed, and angry at myself for being stupid! I promptly threw the gloves away. I didn't even want them anymore. On the way home my mother asked me why I wanted to have a career as a thief once I grew up? I assured her that I didn't. She said she thought that I did and somehow this had to be her fault. She went on to say that thieves have to understand that they will get caught eventually, and must be able to deal with jail time. She said that she was going to help me by letting me see what jail was like. She gave me a five-month punishment! Two months for attempting to steal, and three months for being stupid and bending to peer pressure.

For five months I couldn't go outside the house except to go to school. She also made sure that my grandparents adhered to the time limit. It was torture, but I never attempted stealing again. I also learned to resist peer pressure.

A rod and a reprimand impart wisdom,
but a child left undisciplined disgraces its mother.
- Proverbs 29,15

My mother had a very simple method for teaching us to be trustworthy. If you did something wrong and you told on yourself, the consequences were much lighter than if you did something and then tried to hide it or lie about it.

If and when you did something that you shouldn't have, you would run as fast as you could to confess your wrongdoings before someone else did! In this scenario most times all you got was a stern talking too, but if something happened and she found out about it from another source then the punishments or the once in a blue moon spanking would come.

If something crazy did occur and no one admitted guilt, and no one told on the culprit then everybody had to get a whipping. My mother would usually give only 1-2 light taps to Keisha and I for not telling or not knowing what was going on. She would then proceed to beat the hell out of Tracie and LaFonya (Red). They were always into something and Red would never tell on Tracie. My mother was a stern believer in siblings looking out for each other and trying to hold each other accountable.

Remember that you are not your child's friend. Stop trying to be their friend. You are their parent. You can and should be friendly toward your children, but you are not their friend! While growing up your children may take the position of them against you. Don't be discouraged, it's just them trying to figure out who they are.

Every parent will have a pet peeve. My mother's pet peeve was lying. One of her favorite sayings was "If you lie, you'll steal. If you'll steal, you'll kill". In her mind, she believed that lying was an example of poor character that would eventually lead you to commit theft and finally murder.

I never figured out whether her thinking was flawed or not, but my siblings and I all turned out to be decent law-abiding people without any real problems.

Mom tried to use spanking as a last resort, but when she spanked us, I think it hurt her more than it hurt us. She never knew it, but I've seen her cry a few times after having to spank us. Don't get me wrong if she spanked you, she tried to beat the black off you, but she tried talking and cajoling first. Then she went to punishments and finally to spanking.

Listed here is an excerpt from an article that I thought was appropriate. It was written by Lauren Steele on Why Discipline Helps Kids it was posted Jan 18, 2018, on the website www.fatherly.com:

> *It doesn't usually feel great to <u>discipline</u> your kid. There is often anger, sadness, tension, <u>stress,</u> and sometimes even <u>tears</u>. But proper discipline is one of the most important components of your <u>child's development</u>. Difficult confrontations now will ultimately make life easier for you and, especially, your kid.*

> *In short, discipline is about teaching children a system of values that they can use to guide them through life. This system can lead to a healthier emotional life that promotes the development of self-motivation, self-control, personality, and decision-making processes. In other words, discipline allows children to develop self-discipline and helps them become emotionally and socially mature adults.*

I believe that most if not all parents want the best for their children. Set the ground rules of discipline in your home early. You can't wait until your child is eight to ten years old or older before trying to get them to act accordingly. When it comes to discipline you *MUST* be consistent. Remember that if you don't and won't discipline your child, **life** will.

Do not withhold discipline from a child; if you punish them with the rod, they will not die.

\- Proverbs 23,13

At the end of the day, NO parent is perfect. I'm not perfect and you're not perfect. Try your best to discipline your children in a ***loving*** manner. Don't forget that even if you do everything right, sometimes kids will still go astray.

10. Encourage Their Dreams

Fathers, do not provoke your children, lest they become discouraged.

- Colossians 3,21

For your child's mental, physical, and spiritual wellbeing it is imperative that parents encourage their dreams. As human beings, our achievements to date are a culmination of wherever our dreams have taken us.

Looking back over my own life, I wish that I would have dreamed more and dreamed bigger. I read somewhere that the bigger the dream the bigger the achievement! Help your children have faith in their dreams, whatever they are. Don't limit your children's dreams by distilling their dreams through the lens of your own practicality or experience.

As parents, we all want our children to be happy in life and succeed. We encourage our children to dream big. We nourish our children's dreams. We buy our future fireman a fireman's hat at the toy store and take him to visit the local fire station. We invest in a piano and arrange music lessons for our budding concert pianist. We applaud our yet-to-be-discovered movie star by sending her to drama camp at the local college. We foster our emerging soccer star's ambitions by signing up for a traveling team. There is nothing wrong with helping our children explore their dreams. It's one way of letting them "try on" potential career choices to see how they fit. But some parents become so wrapped up in their children's dreams that they lose perspective and fail to interject a necessary dose of reality.

When they are young, children's dreams change quickly. Today's fireman is tomorrow's astronaut and next week's rock star. But as children grow up, dreams begin to move them toward career paths. Sometimes parents co-opt their children's dreams, reliving their own failed dreams or missed opportunities through their children. The dad who always wanted to be a high school quarterback pushes his son into football. The mom who dreamed of winning the lead in the high school play pressures her daughter into drama.

When parents force their own agenda onto their children's dreams, children suffer. They are torn between their own interest or lack of interest and pleasing their parents. When parents "over-encourage" their children to succeed, particularly if the child expresses disinterest or feels uncomfortable with his ability to compete, children can become anxious. Constant anxiety can lead to insomnia, behavior problems, even depression, and other emotional problems.

Parents need to take a step back and allow children to fully experience their own dreams. Certainly, provide opportunities to explore interests and talents; but temper dreams with reality. If your child warms the bench during the game, don't step in and argue with the coach or make excuses that feed your child's sense of entitlement. Allow your child the important lessons of disappointment and failure.

Finding out for themselves whether they have the ability and skill to realize their dreams helps children to refine and restructure their dreams into attainable goals.

-Marks Psychiatry | Dr. Tracey Marks

11. Teach Them to Fight and Believe

Our children must learn to never give up! Fighting for your place in America is necessary and expected. If our kids are knocked down 10 times then they MUST get up 11 times.

"People might not get all they work for in this world, but they must certainly work for all they get."

\- Frederick Douglass

Dr. Tae Yun Kim says, "If he can do it and she can do it why not me!". I first read that quote almost 30 years ago, and have since tried to live by it. More importantly, I made sure that my kids lived by it. Every time my children get discouraged by life's ups and downs, I would quote that phrase to them and push them a little bit more.

As black parents, we can't afford to raise weak-minded children. Take Dr. Tae Yun Kim listed above. She is a Korean emigrant that remade herself into a self-made millionaire, successful business owner, motivational speaker, and Tae Kwon Do Grandmaster. She started out in life way worse off than most black people in America. She was born to parents who didn't want her because she was born a "worthless girl" (their words) in the aftermath of the Korean War. She almost starved to death as a child since her family only gave food to the ones old enough to work. When she wanted to learn martial arts, no one would teach her because she was a girl. But this woman is a Lion.

She doesn't know how to quit. After persevering she finally found a master to train her and earned master ranks in Tae Kwon Do while still in Korea. She came to America with nothing, not even a decent grasp of the language, but she still succeeded. As parents, we can't accept anything less from our children.

We need to somehow get our children to see that their dreams are not only possible but *attainable*. Let's make sure our children grow up to be *Lions* and not pussycats.

Calvin Coolidge, said, "Nothing in the world can take the place of persistence. Talent will not; Nothing is more common than unsuccessful men with talent. Genius will not; unrewarded genius is also a proverb. Education will not; the world is full of educated derelicts. Persistence and determination alone are omnipotent. The slogan Press On! Has solved and will always solve the problems of the human race."

"The American people love those who stand up for what they believe in, back up their words with actions, and fight for what they want."

-Rev. Romal J. Tune

Fighting for what you want and believing that you'll get it is the immigrant model. Make no mistake African-Americans are children of immigrants. Yes, we are a product of forced immigration, but that doesn't change the fact that the immigration model *will* work for Black Americans as well. We just have to get our children to want it bad enough.

The model that *all* immigrants seem to use is to take advantage of every opportunity and strive to improve their lot in life. Let's remind our children that this is *America, the land of opportunity*. As proof that this opportunity still exists, people from around the world are still flocking to our shores for a chance at the American Dream!

Nowhere is it written that this is the land of opportunity for some and not others. This is America! Opportunity is only limited by our minds. That being said our kids have to take opportunity by the collar and hang on for dear life.

Yes, racism still exists. Yes, black people may not get a fair shake from the courts or police. *So, What*!! My Stepfather gave me a valuable lesson about racism when I was about 10 or 11 years old. I don't remember the exact problem, but almost 50 years later I still remember his response. I competed or applied for something or other and I didn't get it. I complained about it to my stepfather and said I didn't win because I'm black. I thought that they were prejudiced against me. Man, did he set me straight.

He said, "Even if there were prejudicial opinions at play, *So What!* You still have to succeed! You don't know anything about prejudice or racism anyway. Nobody is beating you with hoses or releasing attack dogs on you for just walking down the street. Nobody is telling you where to live or where you can't live. Nobody is telling you what job you can have or how much money you can make regardless of your education."

He added, "Black folks living in this country prior to the 1964 passing of the Civil Rights Act understood racism firsthand. They understood real struggle. Regardless of what life threw at them, they knew that they *had* to succeed! Success meant Life or Death. Here you are with your nice cushy life and having the audacity to complain about racism. *NO MATTER WHAT GETS THROWN AT YOU, SO WHAT! STILL, YOU MUST SUCCEED!*"

Thanks, Dad I never forgot.

The following excerpt from Maya Angelou's poem "Still I Rise" beautifully expresses the importance of not giving up,

Out of the huts of history's shame
I rise
Up from a past, that's rooted in pain
I rise
I'm a black ocean, leaping and wide,

Welling and swelling I bear in the tide.

Leaving behind nights of terror and fear

I rise

Into a daybreak that's wondrously clear

I rise

Bringing the gifts that my ancestors gave,

I am the dream and the hope of the slave.

I rise

I rise

I rise.

The thing that I have found true is that most folks don't care one way or another about your skin color. They just don't want you impacting them or bothering their stuff.

The majority of people who seem to have problems with race don't even know any black people. They are reacting to irrational fears stoked by the uneven portrayal of minorities in mass media, news, movies, etc.

One of the best ways around this is to *persistently* exercise real economic control in mass media. When you can take control of the conversation, perceptions will eventually change.

There have been multiple studies of successful people in all fields. The trait that they all seem to possess is persistence. They get a goal or a dream in their mind and they don't quit until the dream becomes reality.

My mother will never admit it, but she is a dreamer. Growing up she encouraged my siblings and I to dream. I tried doing this with my children during and after their formative years. What this does is allow life's possibilities to become ingrained in your child's spirit.

Nobody does anything worthwhile without a dream or a goal. Myself included. Sometimes we all need a little push when we want to quit. Learn how to give that gentle little nudge to your younger children and be ready to explain the consequences of life's realities to your older children when they want to quit.

Thanks to my dad I've always loved martial arts. Over the years I've been blessed to earn a black belt rank in several martial arts. During my teens and early 20's I was blessed to train under Grandmaster Hwa Chong - Tae Kwon Do. I've trained several other martial arts since then and saw many world-renowned teachers. I can honestly say he is the best teacher I ever saw. He had a knack for figuring out just how to motivate *you*. Different people require different motivational styles to help them get the maximum output out of themselves. Your children are no different! Our job is to figure out what that trigger is for our children.

During my time with Master Chong, I earned a 1st Gup Brown Belt and never tested for Black Belt. About 5-7 years later I ran into Master Chong and he admonished me for not completing the training and at least earning a Black Belt in Korean Martial Arts. He told me that I was smart and had tons of natural ability, but that I had a tendency to quit when things got hard. I was so angry, but it worked!

Now every time I try something different and want to quit, I can hear Master Chong's voice "Phonsoo what are you doing, are you quitting again?" I get mad all over again and trudge on. I can't stand it when someone tells me no, or doesn't think I can do something.

The latest big goal that I achieved prior to writing this book was my earning a Black Belt in Kuk Sool Won in 2014. Kuk Sool Won is a physically intense martial art that includes jumping, tumbling, high kicking, etc. Not something that most folks would start in their mid-40's. Most people earn a Kuk Sool Won Black Belt in 4 - 6 years. It took me almost 11 years. Along the way, I had life challenges like everyone else including, financial stress, family problems, illness, and injury.

I wanted to quit in 2011. I was participating in a semi-private class and my body just quit. I just couldn't move anymore. I was so embarrassed I started to cry. Can you imagine a grown man tearing up like a small child? I wanted to quit that night. On the drive home I made up every excuse to quit, you're too old, you're overweight, you can't afford it, you've got arthritis, you're taking too much time away from your family and career, etc.

When I arrived back at home my new copy of Tae Kwon Do Times had arrived. When I opened the magazine and the first article, I saw was Master Tae Yun Kim talking about not giving up on your goals. Later that night while lying in bed I could hear Master Chong asking me if I was a quitter? Quietly I answered, No I'm not a quitter! A byproduct of me not quitting Kuk Sool Won is my health. I feel much better today at 60 (at the time of this writing) than I did at 50.

"Thanks, Master Chong!"

To me, persistence comes down to courage. The courage to keep pushing, to keep going.

"Courage is the most important of all the virtues because, without courage, you can't practice any other virtue consistently."

- Maya Angelou

---

12. Talk About Bullying

When adults respond quickly and consistently to bullying behavior, they send the message that it is not acceptable. Research shows this can stop bullying behavior over time.

Parents, school staff, and other adults in the community can help kids prevent bullying by talking about it, building a safe school environment, and creating a community-wide bullying prevention strategy.

\- Stopbullying.gov

Bullying was an area that I wasn't able to help my daughter with. She was bullied in elementary school. I did all the things that I believed parents could do. I tried teaching her Budo Taijutsu self-defense, spoke to her teachers and administrators at her school, signed her up for Tae Kwon Do lessons, talked to her about standing up for herself. My wife also tried cajoling, bribing her, fussing, even threatening her.

None of it worked. Bullying was a real problem for her. My daughter told me that Taijutsu and grappling scared her and that the Tae Kwon Do lessons gave her greater anxiety about fighting. She said teachers and administrators were of no help, and us arguing at her made her feel even worse.

I didn't know what to do. I knew that I didn't want to use my mother's method for handling bullies. I remember visiting my mom one summer right before my eighth birthday. The kid downstairs had a problem with his throat and he spoke with a deep bass voice and he was only nine years old, I was more afraid of his voice than anything. He hit me and sent me back upstairs to my mom's flat crying. My mom promptly grabbed my dad's belt and whipped my butt all the way back downstairs and made me fight him until I won. She wasn't going to put up with the consequences of bullying.

Like most kids, we made up and were playing together the next day. The kid I fought asked me why was I crying while whipping his butt the previous day. I couldn't really articulate it to him. But I remember that the more I hit him, the worse it made me feel.

My mom claimed that my middle sister and I were too soft-hearted and much too easy to cry. I remember my mom being so angry and asking why we couldn't be more like Tracie (the oldest of my little sisters) and stand up for ourselves. Tracie is tough and never took anything off of anybody. I don't know if this being so-called "soft-hearted" is a character flaw or not, but over the years this attitude of trying to get along has allowed me to deeply care for others and easily make friends wherever I go.

If your child is timid or just doesn't want to hurt anybody, please don't berate them if they are being bullied. This can only exacerbate the situation. Try teaching your child verbal skills that will enable them to get out of a situation.

The popular phrase for this is called "Verbal Judo". In studies, this has been shown to be effective in certain cases by diffusing a bullying situation before the confrontation becomes physical.

In other cases, your child may just have to fight back. Growing up I had to fight on occasion. I hated it. I was always afraid that I was going to hurt someone. So, if a kid picked on me, I tried everything I could to get out of fighting. I tried walking away and talking my way out of it. I tried declaring the other kid the winner before the fight commenced, also tried convincing the other kid that beating me up would not enhance his reputation, etc. But sometimes you just have to fight!

I believe that I was more afraid that my mother would find out that I didn't stand up for myself than I was of the other children bullying me. My mother was pretty patient about everything except not standing up for yourself. That was another one of her pet peeves.

On a national level violence in schools and bullying in particular have to be addressed. The following stories list my own families struggles with bullying and our solution. What worked for us may not work for your family, but stay vigilant and plugged into your children's lives. If your child is being bullied don't give up!

A bullying incident occurred that changed my whole paradigm about standing up for myself. This happened when I was 8 years old in the 3rd grade. I got into a scuffle with a kid in my class on the way home from school during lunch recess. During the fight, he cut me above my right eye with a flip-top cigarette lighter. I bled all over my jacket and my eye was almost swollen shut. When I got home, I wanted to get medical treatment. My grandmother washed my face, changed my shirt, and put Vaseline over my eye and asked if I could see. Once I affirmatively answered her, she promptly marched me back up to school and had the principal call in the other child's parents for a conference.

On the way back to the school my grandmother proceeded to ask me "how could you be so stupid as to let someone do this to your eye". Being berated was much worse than the injury or any perceived bullying. This injury must have looked way worse than it felt. Even worse was the reactions from teachers, other students, and the office staff. They looked at me squinting, grimacing, looking away, and saying "Oh god.". Being forced to stay in school for the rest of the day. I sat there angry and embarrassed. I then made up my mind to never be in a situation like that ever again. I decided that I was going to stand up for myself to come hell or high water no matter what. I was not going to become a victim of bullying ever again.

On the rare occasions when I had to fight, I fought with everything that I had. Once I made my mind up that I wasn't going to be bullied anymore, I proceeded to fight anywhere - anytime. In class, in church, at the grocery store. It didn't matter, if a kid hit me or threatened to hit me, I would start fighting right then and there.

In my case, once kids knew that I would stand up for myself and had gained limited martial arts experience, I didn't have to fight any more in elementary school. The bullying stopped. That seems to be the case with most bullies. They are looking for the easy mark because the weaker or shy kids won't or can't fight back.

If your child is getting bullied and decides to fight back, be aware that they could flip in the other direction. You have to make sure that your child doesn't morph into the bully. My new attitude about fighting earned me poor citizenship grades in middle school and I proceeded to get into unnecessary fights because I refused to back down.

It got so bad, I almost got expelled from middle school. My dad (stepfather) told me that if he had to take off work and come up to the school, I was going to be sorry. He had only spanked me one time in my entire life and I didn't want any part of a 2nd one.

I spent the first eight days of my high school career at the old Detroit Northern High School. I proceeded to have eight pushing matches and quick scuffles in that short period of time. Most of these were because I refused to shut my mouth or back down. I really needed "Verbal Judo".

I was blessed to transfer and graduate from Detroit Cass Technical High School. This school was Detroit's first magnet school program that attracted kids from all over the city. As such you were so busy with school work that you didn't have time for any foolishness. They also had a no-tolerance policy for any violence or bullying in the school.

When I attended this school there were approximately 4500 students in attendance. There was very little fighting on campus. They ran the school like a college campus and you were expected to act accordingly.

I wish more of our children were exposed to safe school environments. School violence is a hindrance to getting a quality education. Bullying is getting so much notoriety. Government studies look at this problem as a Public Health issue.

Bullying can threaten students' physical and emotional safety at school and can negatively impact their ability to learn. The best way to address bullying is to stop it before it starts. There are a number of things school staff can do to make schools safer and prevent bullying.

Training school staff and students to prevent and address bullying can help sustain bullying prevention efforts over time. There are no federal mandates for bullying curricula or staff training.

\- Stopbullying.gov

I want to state that I don't condone violence. In a perfect world, bullying doesn't happen. The problem is that we live in this world and so does your child. Since we live in this world, sometimes we have to resort to the things this world understands.

I know that this may seem mean or callus, but explain to your child that if they are bullied and another child assaults them, they have nothing to lose by fighting back. There is no excuse for anyone physically assaulting your child. Your child has to know that the worst thing that could happen has already happened - they got bullied! If your child decides to stand up for themselves, it has to be done with enough confidence to get the message across. They at least have to make sure that the bully will pause before picking on them again. They have to stand up with everything they have in them.

Best case scenario, your child fights back and the bully leaves your child alone and goes on to find an easier target elsewhere. Worst case scenario the bullying could escalate. There are no easy answers or one size fits all scenarios when it comes to bullying.

My daughter had finally had enough when she got to be about 10 or 11 years old. My daughter says that she was playing by herself on the playground during school recess. A group of girls her age came over and started taunting her. One of the girls then reached over and tore off the lace bib from my daughter's dress. My daughter's favorite dress at that time. My daughter really went after this girl to the point that a teacher had to pull her off the child. Of course, we were called to the school.

The principal asked us what we were teaching our daughter at home, he said an adult male teacher could barely restrain our daughter from doing great harm to the other student. I'm glad no one was seriously injured, but this seemed kind of ironic after all the visits to the school concerning bullying. My daughter reported that after this incident the bullying stopped. She gained the confidence to stand up for herself.

I interviewed my son and asked him why he thinks he wasn't bullied growing up. My son said, "Dad there are some things that I just can't put up with, and people attempting to put me down is one of them. I would stand up for myself if I had too without even thinking about it".

In the cases of myself, my son, and my daughter, our experiences showed that bullying will cease if your child has the courage to stand up for themselves. This may be easier said than done, and depending on the type of bullying - things could easily escalate.

Be aware that bullying can come in many forms, it can be physical assaults, verbal intimidation, or social media tormenting. For children in the information age, social media bullying is the worst and most dangerous because it can be invisible to parents. Children that are not intimidating in person can be tyrants behind the safety of a keyboard or text message.

There is no easy one size fits all solution when it comes to bullying. There will be consequences and fall-out whether your child stands up for themselves or not. Be sure to get involved whether your child is being bullied or is the bully. Know that your child is not alone. The problem is also bigger than your local school or your town.

State and local lawmakers have taken action to prevent bullying and protect children.[1] Each jurisdiction, including all 50 states, the District of Columbia, and U.S. territories (state), addresses bullying differently. Some have established laws, policies, and regulations.[2] Others have developed model policies schools and local educational agencies (districts) can use as they develop their own local laws, policies, and regulations. Most state laws, policies, and regulations require districts and schools to implement a bullying policy and procedures to investigate and respond to bullying when it occurs. A handful of states also require bullying prevention programs, inclusion of bullying prevention in health education standards, and or teacher professional development. These state laws generally do not prescribe specific consequences for kids who engage in bullying behavior, and very few classify bullying as a criminal offense. Further, states may address bullying, cyberbullying, and related behaviors in a single law or across multiple laws. In some cases, bullying appears in the criminal code of a state that may apply to juveniles

- **Stopbullying.gov**

As you can see there are no easy answers to bullying. Some kids will respond to self-defense training. Other children will become experts at "Verbal Judo", still others may respond with sports participation to gain self confidence, etc. No matter what vehicle works for your child, be sure to fully support and encourage your child. Don't berate them, support them! The idea here is to find out what will work for your child to get them to make up their mind to not take it anymore!

To be successful in life, our children must learn to stand up for themselves. Our job as parents is to figure out how to instill that inner confidence into our kids.

13. Talk to Your Children About Finances

Financial responsibility is a cornerstone of success in America. Without adequate Financial Resources, there's not a lot that you can enjoy here in America. I'm not saying that you can't be successful without money but let's face the facts, money is the great equalizer. I know some of our parents and grandparents have taught that being poor is a virtue. In some instances that may be true, but here in America, our whole society is built around having adequate finances.

Surprisingly, many businessmen and women seemed to feel guilty about the whole idea of prosperity, though they were working quite hard to become prosperous, day in and day out, in their respective professions. But the question remained in their minds, Is poverty a spiritual virtue or a common vice? This discord in their thinking was creating a tug-of-war in their affairs which neutralized their efforts to succeed, no matter how much work they put forth Be done with the thinking of poverty as a virtue---it is a common vice! This is the shocking truth about poverty!

-Excerpted from Think and Grow Rich - A Black Choice by Dennis Kimbro and Napoleon Hill

At some point in everyone's life in order to enjoy all the benefits of America, you have to have money. I'm not saying money is everything but it's a great tool. You can't build a house without nails and you can't build a house without a hammer either. These are some of the tools a Builder needs to build a house. Money is one of the tools that our children need to build a successful life and have access to everything that America offers.

Growing up, my parents and grandparents didn't talk to us about finances very often. Yes, I heard the occasional *"you need to save money."*. But this didn't tell me the why, how, or what amount. Also, I didn't **see** my family save very much, so I fell into consumerism just like most Americans. Remember our kids learn as much by watching us as well as listening.

If your family is having financial challenges, it's not the end of the world. You need to become a student of finances. A must-read is the book, *"The Millionaire Next Door"* written by Thomas J Stanley & William D Danko.

Their research suggests that over 80% of millionaires in America earn less than $100,000 per year. The examples in their book give us proof that a higher standard of living is possible for everyone, and true wealth goals are attainable with the use of true financial knowledge. It will not be easy, but it is attainable. Let your kids see you save and invest. Discuss your saving and investment strategies with them. This is *very* important. Remember to start as early as possible.

Money Magazine is a great resource in learning basic terms on saving and the investing strategies of real people. You owe it to yourself to read Dennis Kimbro's masterpiece on wealth creation and a positive mindset - Think and Grow Rich - A Black Choice. The following is an eye-opening excerpt from Think and Grow Rich - A Black Choice by Dennis Kimbro and Napoleon Hill,

> *Black Americans earn $350 billion in annual income (estimated at $900 billion by the year 2000) and spend $225 billion a year on goods and services. This dollar figure is equivalent to the gross national product of Canada or Australia, two of the ten largest nations in the free world. Black America's problem is not a lack of money; its problems stem from what it does with the money it has.*

That was written in 1991. Since then America has created several famous black billionaires like Robert L. Johnson, Oprah Winfrey, Michael Jordan, and Tiger Woods. The idea that wealth is attainable in America is as American as apple pie. Yes, there may still be other barriers to black wealth that our white counterparts may not have to deal with, but SO WHAT! We can't stop or sit back and wait for life to be fair.

Life will never be 100% fair. For a large part of his career playing for the Chicago Bulls, Michael Jordan wasn't even the highest-paid player on the team. Think about the unfairness of that.

During that time, he was considered the best player on the planet! He didn't stop. He just went out and did his best by winning six championships and securing a merchandising contract with Nike that as of this writing is still paying him hundreds of millions of dollars well past his playing days.

He has been super successful because he chose to constantly expand his financial knowledge. Learning about finance is critical to your child's long-term success and quality of life.

My mother and my in-laws were savers. The big difference was that my mother kept it hidden and didn't teach us about saving. When my in-laws retired and saw that the family as a whole was not saving anything, they started shouting from the rafters the importance of saving. This had a big impact on my son.

My in-laws were my son's primary caregivers and sitters until he was four years old. Consequently, he became a saver. He so strongly believed in saving that as a child he would cry if he had to spend any of his savings.

They had given him an old wallet to carry around when he was two years old! He would take his money and put it in his piggyback and come back showing me his empty wallet. When I inquired as to why he was showing me an empty wallet he would promptly ask for more money to put in it. "Grandad said a man ain't supposed to leave home with an empty wallet" - that quote is from my then two-year-old son.

Saving and investing is contagious. Once you start seeing the balances grow, your excitement about your saving and investing will also grow. If you share this feeling of accomplishment with your children, they will get excited as well. Remember, pennies make dollars, dollars make hundreds, hundreds make thousands, and eventually, thousands make millions.

The dangers of excessive consumerism are real. I've seen it first hand in my sales career over and over again. Customers coming in to buy big-ticket items and unable to come up with $500, even though they have salaries in excess of $100,000 per year.

Doing research for this book I've noticed that financially successful people consistently live below their means and try to earmark their excess earnings into investing and starting businesses. Then as those investments and businesses mature, they use the *profit* proceeds to buy homes, cars, etc. Everyone else uses these large salaries to buy more stuff, but end up with nothing in the long run.

Financial responsibility is a stalwart of America. Let us make sure that our children don't fall into the trap of having successful careers, but no money. Excessive consumerism and debt are a snare that has captured most working Americans.

Give your children the knowledge to avoid such traps. Even if you have fallen into the debt trap yourself, be willing to share that with your teenagers and preteens giving real-world examples of what not to do. This is nothing to be ashamed of. Just be sure to come up with some type of long-term plan to pull yourself out of debt.

14. Ninja Mindset

Growing up I loved reading about the exploits of the Ninja. Faced with seemingly insurmountable odds they always seemed to come through. I believe that it was Stephen Hayes who coined the phrase - "Ninjutsu is the art of winning.". As parents, we must be like the ninja and learn to win at all costs when it comes to our children.

I didn't always get along with my mother while growing up, but I always admired her ability to persevere through just about anything. She was just like the Ninja in the storybooks. Looking back, it was her attitude that kept us going. One of her favorite sayings was, *"just because we live in the ghetto, doesn't mean the ghetto has to live inside you"*. This was a warning to keep our attitudes right and to stay positive.

As parents, you should expect that life is going to throw curveball after curveball. So be ready to bat when we step up to the plate. Parenthood is not for the weak of heart, and nobody said that it would be.

The spring and summer of 1974 gave our family a huge test. My mother had no income and the welfare office refused to give us any aid because my stepfather made too much money. My mother had explained to the welfare office that he no longer lived there, and when he left his income left with him. My mother was told about some stupid rule that my stepfather had to be out of the house for a minimum amount of time before we would be eligible for aid.

That was one of the few times I ever saw my mother look beaten. It lasted for about 10 minutes. Afterward, she stood up, straightened her back, and pieced together a strategy. She visited the caretaker letting him know about our plight and when he could expect the next rent payment. She then had me collect all of our piggy banks to assess our cash situation. At that time my sisters (ages 8, 6, and 3) had some of those big plastic piggy banks (approx. 2 feet tall).

We found that we had over $100. Like most teenagers, I started to panic. Not about our pending doom and possible starvation, but worrying about how I was going to have money to hang out with my friends. Thankfully my mom didn't try to kill me! She just sent me to the store to buy hot dogs and buns.

Speaking of hotdogs. My mother made a deal with the local market to sell us the old hot dogs before they were to be thrown out. Some of these hot dogs were blue or had white slime and mold growing on them. They were terrible. We were able to buy 24 hot dogs for a dollar. We did this every few days. We couldn't afford the buns anymore, but mom got creative. She washed the slime off those hot dogs and made a meal. We ate grilled hot dogs, boiled hotdogs, baked hot dogs, fried hot dogs, hotdogs with fries, hotdogs with rice, hot dogs with spaghetti, hot dogs with soup, hotdogs with oatmeal, cornbread hot dogs, hotdogs on a stick, cheese hot dogs. She even tried cinnamon hot dogs once when we wanted something sweet. Yeah, we didn't have much variety but we survived and made it through!

Whenever my sisters or I would complain about the food or our lack of something that we wanted, my mother would make us play games and visualize something better. I remember her having us stand over the gas stove and grill the hotdogs over the fire. She had us visualize that we were on a camping trip and the eye of the stove was a campfire. She even had us sing songs. My mother did *anything* she had to do for us to survive.

I'm not going to tell you everything was great and that it always worked out. It didn't. It was tough back then.

The "nin" symbol 忍 of ninjutsu can mean to endure or persevere. The ancient ninja not only trained in physical skills but mental skills as well. They would visualize and chant mantras over and over again to get themselves mentally ready to do whatever job they were supposed to do. Failure was not an option.

Sometimes being a parent is a thankless job. If you get any thanks at all, it may come later when your children are adults, it may never come at all! Being a good parent is all about enduring. Failure is not an option for you either.

What I didn't tell you about the hot dog story was that while all that was going on, my sisters and I were actually mad at my mother for making my stepfather move out. Can you believe it? We should have been mad at him for trying to punish my mom and us financially for his mistakes. The only thing that got my mother through these ordeals was her mental attitude and toughness. Her ability to constantly tell herself over and over again that everything is going to be alright.

To raise successful children here in America regardless of your ethnicity you *must* maintain a positive mental attitude and be willing to persevere through life's trials. You can't just quit and throw in the towel, even if you want too. Your babies need you to fight on. Your family's future along with your own depends on it.

"Even when you are faced with certain death, die laughing!"
- Toshitsgu Takamatsu
Last of the true ninja fighters b.3- 10- 1887 - d.4- 2-
1972

The previous quote by Takamatsu is taken out of context here but I believed that parenting is that serious. The difference between good parenting and bad parenting can at some point come down to life or death for your child.

At this point in time in America, it seems that we are stuck in an atmosphere of negative influences and fear. To prevent this negative power from damaging and stunting our children's mental growth, we must present a paradigm of positive energy.

In order to exude positive energy or teach a positive lifestyle to our children, we have to train our own mental energy. Luckily, today no one is running around trying to hack us up with a sword, but like the ninja of old, we need to constantly place positive energy into our souls.

This input of positive energy into our spirits will allow us to face life's little ups and downs with confidence. It will allow us to smile and persevere.

"A big smile gives you confidence. A big smile beats fear, rolls away worry, defeats despondency."
- David J. Schwartz, Ph.D. - The Magic of Thinking Big

Okay, you're probably asking how to do it. Quite simply take advantage of all the positive thinking, self-help materials available to you. A lot of it is free or low cost online. If you want to change the trajectory of your life and improve your children's future, put some positive affirmations into your spirit *every* day!

15. Talk About Drug and Alcohol Abuse

I'm sharing my family's and extended family's struggles with drug and alcohol abuse in hopes that it will give you the push to talk to your children about the devastating effects of this abuse. I know that these stories will open some old wounds for my family and for that I'm sorry. But if it can help just one family avoid drug and alcohol abuse it is worth the pain.

Remember, our children will do as we do instead of doing as we tell them. If you are a recreational drug user don't do it around your kids. If you like to drink excessively and get smashed on the weekends, your kids shouldn't see you like this. Seeing my mom occasionally use marijuana and my dad drinking all the time made this behavior somehow seem alright. You *must* keep this behavior away from your children.

> *The risk of developing drug and alcohol problems is higher in children whose parents abuse alcohol or drugs—but it is NOT a guarantee. Research shows that children with parents who abuse alcohol or drugs are more likely to try alcohol or drugs and develop alcoholism or drug addiction. Why?*

● Children whose parents abuse alcohol and drugs are more likely to have behavioral problems, which increases the risk of trying alcohol or drugs. They are also exposed to more opportunities to try these substances.

● Plus, children of parents who abuse drugs may inherit a genetic predisposition (or greater likelihood) for addiction—having an "addictive personality," so to speak.

Of course, most children of parents who abuse alcohol or drugs do not develop alcoholism or addiction themselves, so your genes do not write your destiny to become addicted to drugs. BUT to avoid that risk entirely, it's best not to start...

- National Institute on Drug Abuse for Teens

I was blessed to have real-world examples of drug and alcohol abuse in both my family and extended family. This made it easy to talk to my children about these subjects. Also, having examples close at hand made the dangers of drug and alcohol abuse undeniable to my children.

People use drugs for many reasons, they want to feel good, stop feeling bad, or perform better in school or at work, or they are curious because others are doing it and they want to fit in. The last reason is very common among teens. At first, taking drugs is usually your choice. But as you continue to take them, using self-control can become harder and harder; this is the biggest sign of addiction. Brain studies of people with addiction show physical changes in parts of the brain that are very important for judgment, making decisions, learning and memory, and controlling behavior.

Scientists have shown that when this happens to the brain, it changes how the brain works and it explains the harmful behaviors of addiction that are so hard to control.

- National Institute on Drug Abuse

Looking back on the marriage of my mom and dad (stepfather) I could be looking through the rose-colored glasses of my youth. My maternal grandmother (Miss Ann) demanded that I live with her and not my mother. Hence as a child, I only spent weekends and summer vacations with my mom, dad, and sisters.

My dad was a *great* parent, but a terrible husband to my mom. He only wanted to do things with and for the kids. My mom would suggest something that they could do as a couple and he would shoot it down if it didn't involve the children. I never got around to asking why he was that way.

His alcohol consumption slowly went from heavy drinking to full-blown alcoholism. While drinking, his amorous behavior would get out of control. During that time, I don't think that he ever met a woman he didn't like. He tried dating the neighbors, family friends, his friend's wives, etc. My mother finally had enough when he got her teenage cousin pregnant. This destroyed my mother's bond with her extended family. She never spoke to any of her maternal cousins again.

At the time of this writing, it has been almost 50 years since the disintegration of our extended family. Think about all the family gatherings, picnics, parties, graduations, and milestones of life that were missed due to alcohol abuse and shame.

My Dad's drinking not only took an emotional toll on the family but an economic one as well. The old saying of *"when it rains it pours"* defines our family life around this time. Shortly after my parent's marriage broke up another tragedy struck. All of our family get-togethers and celebrations up to this point revolved around my maternal grandmother Miss Ann. She had a massive heart attack and passed away. Around the same time, my dad lost his job at Ford Motor Company due to his drinking.

After my grandmother died my grandfather started drinking Gin. Up to that point, the strongest thing he ever drank was cola. On top of all this, my grandfather announces that I'd have to move in with my mother because he couldn't look after me anymore.

My grandfather quit his job at General Motors after 29 years and then sued the company. This destroyed his pension. He then promptly moved out of his and my grandmother's home. During his move, all our family's heirlooms, pictures, and memorabilia were lost or thrown away. My grandfather and my mother had a disagreement about my grandmother's funeral due to his drinking and acting erratic. Subsequently, my mother wasn't allowed to collect any of her mother's items such as our baby pictures, from my grandparents' home.

All this turmoil and upheaval gave me a first-hand view of my mother's parenting resourcefulness. We went from a solid functioning middle class working family to a dysfunctional financially destitute family overnight largely due to excess alcohol consumption.

Wine is a mocker and beer a brawler; whoever is led astray by them is not wise.

- Proverbs 20,1

I believe that my mother's attitude of winning and surviving at any cost got us through. She sat down with my siblings and I and explained that there would be some changes in our lives going forward. Our ages at the time were 14, 7, 5, and 2. I know that my siblings didn't have a clue what mom was talking about, but I was devastated. *"We're going to have to get on the welfare?"* I asked I couldn't believe that this was happening to us.

My being embarrassed about using food stamps wasn't the worst. The thing I was most uneasy about was my friend's acceptance of our poverty. In this land of plenty, we can't be complacent or accepting of poverty.

Alcohol abuse has a well-known economic impact on families. Look at the following U.S. Government Public Health Report from Nov-Dec 1988 (103(6), 564–568),

The economic effects of alcohol abuse are as damaging to the nation as the health effects, affecting the family, the community, and persons of all ages. Underaged drinking is interfering with children's development, affecting the nation's ability to respond to economic challenges in the future. The college-aged may be the most difficult to educate about alcohol abuse because of drinking patterns established at an early age and susceptibility to advertising inducements. Healthcare costs for families with an alcoholic member are twice those for families without one, and up to half of all emergency room admissions are alcohol-related. Fetal alcohol syndrome is one of the top three known causes of birth defects and is totally preventable. Alcohol abuse and alcoholism are estimated to have cost the nation $117 billion in 1983, while nonalcoholic drug abuse that year cost $60 billion. Costs of alcohol abuse are expected to be $136 billion a year by 1990, mostly *from lost productivity and employment. Between 6 and 7 million workers are alcoholic, with an undetermined loss of productivity, profits, and competitiveness of American business. Alcohol abuse contributes to the high healthcare costs of the elderly beneficiaries of Federal health financing programs. Heavily affected minorities include blacks, Hispanics, and Native Americans. Society tends to treat the medical and social consequences of alcohol abuse, rather than its causes. Although our experience with the consequences of alcohol abuse is greater than that for any other drug, public concern for its prevention and treatment is less than for other major illnesses or abuse of other drugs.*

I'm not trying to be overcritical about alcohol consumption. Drinking alcohol is both legally and socially acceptable in *moderation*. The key phrase here is *"in moderation"*. During my early twenties, I drank very heavily. God just blessed me to grow out of it before the advent of children. Explain to your kids that excessive alcohol consumption can be detrimental to their family, finances, relationships, career and that it exacts a physical toll as well. I personally developed prostate issues by my early thirties.

After being thoroughly interviewed and examined by my physician he determined that my early-onset prostate issues were related to excessive alcohol consumption from my 20's.

Share with your children any real-world examples of drug or alcohol abuse that has personally touched you or someone that you know. Doing this puts the dangers of this abuse front and center. Don't be embarrassed or ashamed of a family member's struggle with drug and alcohol addiction or abuse. Don't make excuses for family members or friends that abuse drugs or alcohol. Don't attempt to hide it from your kids. Remember, you have to make your kids *see* and *understand* the relationship fallout and the physical and emotional toll that alcohol and or drug abuse exacts on someone.

Don't forget that your kids learn more by watching you and your behaviors than by what you tell them. If you find yourself imbibing excessive amounts of alcohol don't share that experience with your children. It doesn't help your parental authority one bit by having your children see you drunk, passed out, or acting belligerent from bouts of drinking.

Remember that you are not your child's friend. We want to be friendly with our children, but we can never be their friend. We must be their parent first, before anything else. For me, this meant no drinking and partying with my kids around. I have seen a few families drinking and partying with their teens. After this, the parental authority sailed right out the window.

Thanks to the opioid crisis in America, drug addiction has been brought to the forefront of the news and our national conversation. Drug Addiction struck my extended family extremely hard and left many emotional scars on me as well. From the ages, 16 through 50, my most favorite person in the world was my brother-in-law, Larry. He was one year older than me. The first 7 years I knew my brother-in-law he was the most dependable and fun-loving person I knew. Everyone who knew us thought that I was his younger brother.

He even made sure that my future wife (his sister) didn't have any other suitors. If anyone tried to come around, he would threaten to beat them up and chase them away. He would laugh and say "Hey Bro I'm saving Debra for you; she is going to be your wife". Debby would get really angry and complain to her mom and then threaten to stop speaking to me.

During this period of time, my brother-in-law's bigger than life personality always made him the life of the party and a lot of fun to be around. He would sometimes call me up and say "hey man I'm leaving some money here at the house for you, come on over and take Debra out. You guys go and have some fun."

He taught me how to work on cars, complete basic home repairs, etc. We would often laugh together and dream about all the things that we were going to do, and the places that we would visit as old men in retirement. We really were more like brothers than brothers-in-law. During this period Larry was the kind of guy that you could always count on. No matter whether you need help working on a car, repairing something around the house, needing extra money for something, or help with a scrap. He was a very dependable guy.

Late fall 1979 everything started going topsy-turvy for my future brother-in-law. He was involved in a serious car accident. His first wife was killed along with his unborn child. He was in the hospital off and on for over a month. The accident seemed to push him over the edge. Once he recovered, he started experimenting with narcotics (cocaine) in early 1980 and started developing anger issues.

It is ironic that he would start using cocaine. At that time, I was always considered the crazy one who would try any and everything. I almost flipped my car over on the freeway drinking and driving on one occasion. Also, I constantly smoked excessive amounts of marijuana during this period. When free-base hit Detroit hard in 1979 I was excited and wanted to try it right away. My future brother-in-law warned me to stay away from that "crap" and would "beat me senseless if he even heard someone talking about me even trying free-base cocaine". Since I was a little afraid of my future brother-in-law, I never touched it.

Immediately after his first wife was killed, he met and married another young lady who unfortunately had a brother who was a drug addict and in a motorcycle club. These relationships would have devastating results for everyone involved.

It is not my intention to disparage motorcycle clubs. I don't know anything about them. What I do know is Larry's recreational drug use and overall recklessness skyrocketed while in the motorcycle club environment.

He started experimenting with so-called hard drugs. He also started riding his bike in a more reckless manner. I guess that's what's called trick riding. Wheelies, standing on the seat while riding, etc. This so-called trick riding is fine except you can't do it while high, and this is for experienced riders only.

This recklessness and drug use caused him to have another major accident. This time on his motorcycle. At the time of the accident he had been riding approximately two seasons (can't ride year-round in Michigan). He was riding 90 miles an hour on a city street and hit a car that pulled out in front of him.

This time he was in the hospital for almost five months and was in a full-body cast from the neck down including both arms and legs. He looked like a cartoon character while in that hospital room covered by casts on his arms and legs while hanging in traction. He broke everything in his body except his fingers and his neck.

While confined to the hospital Larry's wife continued to supply him with illegal drugs. He was discharged from the hospital still in a body cast and also hooked on drugs. We chided Larry's wife about providing him drugs and she just shrugs and says "If I don't buy food, I'm going to buy my weed". As he recovered the family noticed that something was a little off about Larry's behavior.

My daughter was a young child while these family dynamics were going on. She sees her uncle go from funny and fun-loving uncle Larry to crazy violent uncle Larry. First comes the violence. He attempts to put his wife's head through a plaster wall because she attempts to stop him from taking the floor model TV out of the house while she and the kids are watching television. He is constantly beating his wife about money that he wants or claims that he needs for the drug man.

The violence escalated until she had a nervous breakdown. This breakdown was precipitated by Larry getting high, tying his wife up. Placing her in the street and attempting to run over her with the family car. This was so outrageous neither I nor the rest of the family knew what to do or say.

The family tried various rehabs and interventions, nothing seemed successful long term. My father-in-law told me that he had spent over $100,000 on Larry over the years trying to keep him out of trouble and alive. He had paid for multiple rehabs and other programs to try to get Larry clean.

Nothing seemed to work long term. He would get off drugs for months at a time and then go back to them.

During this time various drug dealers running to his mom and dad's home demanding money seemed almost the norm. On one occasion my other brother-in-law and I had to go to a crack house to rescue Larry. He was being held hostage until his drug bill was paid. I was so angry and afraid that he put his extended family in such a predicament. If something would have gone wrong, I wouldn't be here writing this book today.

By the time my son was born in 1993, Larry had become a full-fledged functional drug addict and woman abuser. He held various full-time jobs and even completed welding school, but when he was high, he was quite dangerous. Over the years the extended family tried everything in reason in an attempt to bring some normalcy to Larry and his family. All to no avail.

The tragedy of Larry's drug addiction wasn't the pain and suffering the extended family faced. It was the pain, mental anguish, and embarrassment that he caused his children and the women he dated over the years.

The events listed here are true, I wish that I was making up these events. The mother of his youngest children would frequently have busted lips and two black eyes. He even stabbed her in the foot with a pitchfork once. This young lady was a crack addict who abused alcohol as well. Both their children were born with crack cocaine in their systems and both display symptoms of fetal alcohol syndrome.

The next girlfriend was repeatedly beaten and he even attached her with his Rottweiler because she wouldn't give him the bill money for drugs. She was even beaten by Larry's grown children over an overdue drug bill. She finally had had enough and left when he shot the wall above her head with a shotgun while she was sitting and holding Larry's youngest child in her lap. Plaster raining down on her and the baby's heads. Another young lady he moved in shortly there-after had some really nice furniture. After a few months, he put her out and sold all her furniture. He claimed that she was gay and deserved it.

The last relationship he was in before he died was the most tragic. He constantly beat "Jac". Caused her to get fired from her job. Stabbed her. Shot her on two separate occasions and precipitated in the state removing her children and his children out of the home. I know that this sounds like a horror movie, but these events did happen and many more too numerous to mention here.

Drug and alcohol abuse is devastating to everyone involved. Due to drugs, my brother-in-law had a stroke and heart attack 11 months before he died. The doctor warned him that if continued use of drugs it would kill him.

I spoke to him on several occasions about quitting drugs. He asked me "Al have you ever used crack?". When I answered no he said, "then you don't know what you are talking about, when I die you will have to pry the crack pipe from my hands". This was such an illogical response I didn't speak to him about his addiction again. He had a massive heart attack a few months later caused by crack cocaine.

At the time of this writing, he has been dead for almost eight years, and I guess I'm still angry at him for being so reckless and with such bizarre behavior. What's sad is despite the extended family trying to help, his youngest children ended up in the Foster Care system as teens.

Drug addiction snuffed out the life of a fun-loving happy go lucky person and replaced that person with a dangerous caricature of that person. Once when my daughter was talking to my son telling him how much fun uncle Larry was when she was a young child. My son was shocked. His whole life he only saw crazy and reckless uncle Larry.

Talk to your kids about drug and alcohol abuse. Alcohol abuse robbed me of a happy childhood. Drug addiction robbed me of my best friend. Pray that you don't have to live through what I witnessed and lived through. Life is too short. Stress to your children that drug and alcohol abuse is a dead-end!!

16. Encourage Healthy Lifestyles and Fitness

"Do the best you can until you know better. Then when you know better, do better"

- Maya Angelou

Black America has a tradition of sports domination during our youth. After the playing years are over, we become couch potatoes or weekend warriors at best - myself included. As we age this lack of a healthy lifestyle is decimating both Black America and America at large.

In my opinion, Americans don't seem as robust as our fore-parents. This is even more evident for African Americans who have higher incidences of diabetes, obesity, and hypertension per capita than any other group in America.

Modern America is beset with a more sedentary lifestyle. Prior to the Industrial Revolution, our society was agrarian in nature and required hard back-breaking work from sun up to sundown. This hard - physical labor insured a higher base level of fitness which enforced healthier lifestyles.

Modern science subscribes to vegetable-rich diets for longevity and overall health. During times of a more agrarian lifestyle, the diet would have been rich in vegetables. Per my grandfather, this vegetable-heavy diet was not by choice but a necessity. He told me that rural families often couldn't afford much meat so you ate mostly beans, greens, peas, and vegetables with a little meat sprinkled in for flavoring. He said that most times if you wanted meat, you had to hunt for it. My grandfather told me many times "if you didn't catch something, you didn't eat nothing".

All I know is that growing up on a farm and walking almost everywhere as an adult made my grandfather extremely fit with a powerfully built physique. In my opinion, his healthy lifestyle growing up greatly influenced his quality of life in his later years.

The following story is an example of my grandfather's robustness. He used to love going to card parties at his friends the Taylor's. They also had grandchildren around my age so I loved to follow my grandfather over there. I was between the ages of 3 and 5 years old at the time, estimating my weight between 30 - 45 pounds (13.6 – 20.412 kilograms). We lived a little less than 8 miles (12.875 kilometers) from the Taylors. I would poop out after walking about 2 - 3 miles (3.219 – 4.828 kilometers). It was nothing for grandfather to scoop me up onto his shoulders and walk the rest of the way.

Even as a small child I was always amazed at how robust my grandfather was. During that time my grandfather was in his late 40's –

126

early 50's. I firmly believe that by instilling a foundation of healthy lifestyles in our children early on will go a long way towards improving their overall quality of life in their later years. My grandfather lived to be 88 years old. He didn't start getting sick until he was almost 86 years old.

Since African Americans are a microcosm of America at large, a sedentary lifestyle and love affair with fast food does not bode well for America as a whole.

The death rate for African Americans was generally higher than whites for heart diseases, stroke, cancer, asthma, influenza and pneumonia, diabetes, HIV/AIDS, and homicide.

- U.S. Department of Health and Human Services -
Office of Minority Health

A troubling trend has come to my attention. Children here in America (especially boys) don't want to play outside anymore. Everyone wants to stay inside and play video games instead of being active outdoors. I noticed this trend developing over twenty years ago with my oldest nieces and nephews.

Even my son tried to fall into the trap of inactivity when he was approximately 8-9 years old. This occurred during a beautiful sunny summer day. I made him turn off the video game console and go outside to play. Of course, he complained all the way.

My children are eight years apart in age. The oldest being my daughter. There were some things that I didn't get quite right for my daughter, but I was able to tweak them for my son. One of those things was instilling in him an all-around healthy lifestyle and the importance of physical fitness while he was still quite young.

When my daughter reached middle school and high school, she decided to play competitive basketball. She ended up being pretty good too.

My son always tried to prove that he could do anything that his older sister could do. So, he wanted to play basketball as well. Between the two of them, our family life revolved around basketball for 7-8 years. Once my daughter graduated high school, I don't think she thought about basketball again.

By the time my son was in high school his growth spurts really slowed down so he switched to track and field. Track seemed to be his niche. Even earning track scholarships for college. Even though my daughter was more physically gifted than my son, her lack of a fitness foundation as a youngster seemed to hinder her ability to adapt to the rigors of the required physical training needed for competitive sports. I don't believe that this would have been the case if she could have started early building a higher base fitness level.

We really started hammering home the importance of a healthy lifestyle with my son early on. We started talking to him about the challenges our family faced with the understanding and consumption of proper nutrition when he was around two years old.

By the time he was four years old, he was starting to pay attention and ask questions pertaining to proper nutrition. He even started asking for veggies. When he was around eight years old, I asked him why he was so fond of vegetables. He said, "Dad I don't even like vegetables that much but I know that they are necessary".

At the time of this writing, my son is in his late 20's still going to the gym as part of his healthy lifestyle. In my immediate family, he is the only one who never struggled with weight issues.

The only difference between my kids' upbringing was trying to steer my son to a healthier lifestyle while he was still a toddler. A healthy lifestyle is so important as we age.

Look at what the U.S. Department of Health and Human Services has to say on the subject:

Your food choices each day affect your health — how you feel today, tomorrow, and in the future.

Good nutrition is an important part of leading a healthy lifestyle. Combined with physical activity, your diet can help you to reach and maintain a healthy weight, reduce your risk of chronic diseases (like heart disease and cancer), and promote your overall health.

Unhealthy eating habits have contributed to the obesity epidemic in the United States: about one-third of U.S. adults (33.8%) are obese and approximately 17% (or 12.5 million) of children and adolescents aged 2—19 years are obese.1 Even for people at a healthy weight, a poor diet is associated with major health risks that can cause illness and even death. These include heart disease, hypertension (high blood pressure), type 2 diabetes, osteoporosis, and certain types of cancer. By making smart food choices, you can help protect yourself from these health problems.

The risk factors for adult chronic diseases, like hypertension and type 2 diabetes, are increasingly seen in younger ages, often a result of unhealthy eating habits and increased weight gain. Dietary habits established in childhood often carry into adulthood, so teaching children how to eat healthy at a young age will help them stay healthy throughout their life.

The link between good nutrition and a healthy weight greatly reduces chronic disease risk. Overall health is too important to ignore. By taking steps to eat healthily, you'll be on your way to getting the nutrients your body needs to stay healthy, active, and strong. As with physical activity, making small changes in your diet can go a long way, and it's easier than you think!

A healthy lifestyle should include a balance between physical, mental, and spiritual. Each facet of health is no more important than the other. Each area of your child's health is interdependent on the other.

I know that for some parents, speaking to your kids about proper nutrition and healthy lifestyles will be awkward and may even seem hypocritical. It was for me. At the time when I started talking to my son about the importance of a healthy lifestyle, I was 80 pounds (36.287 kilograms) above what I weighed as a newlywed 14 years prior.

Trying to pass on information about healthy lifestyles is a worldwide phenomenon. This idea is bigger than just African American culture or American culture in general. Look at the following excerpt from the Irish website Safefood (www.safefood.eu):

> *A healthy lifestyle has both short and long-term health benefits. Long-term, eating a balanced diet, taking regular exercise, and maintaining a healthy weight can add years to your life and reduce the risk of certain diseases including cancer, diabetes,*

cardiovascular disease, osteoporosis, and obesity. In the short-term, it can also make you feel and look your best, give you more energy, and help you maintain a healthy weight.

The key to reducing the risk of these diseases is making small changes to your daily lives - eating healthier food, getting your 5-a-day, having treats occasionally, and taking more exercise. Improving your lifestyle with small steps in the right direction will have a big impact on your well-being.

Just like the previous passage states if we can instill in our children the importance of continued exercise and healthy eating, the long-term benefits will go a long way toward our children's well-being during their youth and adulthood.

17. Teach Your Children to Cherish What They Have

My professional career has afforded me the opportunity to observe the interaction of hundreds of families both in a professional environment and inside their homes. There seems to be a startling negative attitude of children toward where they live, their parent's automobiles, and their own personal possessions and total disregard for the importance of their home, its surroundings, and their possessions.

This was the case across a wide swatch of socio-economic levels. The working poor, lower middle class, as well as upper-middle-class families. Children seemed to have a total disregard for the sacrifices their parents made to afford them whatever lifestyle the family has achieved.

Early on, I saw this with my own child (my oldest) when she was very young. This forced my wife and I to step it up when it came to explaining the realities of life to my children. We made sure that they understood the value of things and that there is a price to pay in order to live a certain lifestyle.

Sometimes it was as simple as showing them the difference between our home and a like-sized home in an undesirable neighborhood. Other times it was denying a replacement item for an item that was carelessly broken. At times this was hard because as parents you love your children and want to give them all the things that you didn't have as a child. But your child must appreciate what they have, and understand that their possessions *must* be taken care of.

In my own case, I was extremely spoiled until the age of 5. I must have had 12 or more tricycles and bicycles between the ages of 3 and 5 years old. I would keep them for a few weeks until I was tired of the color or something. I would proceed to destroy my bikes. I beat them with hammers. Tossed them repeatedly from the upstairs porch to the sidewalk below until they eventually broke. I even placed them behind the car tire so that they could get crushed when my parents and grandparents were backing the car out.

My mother had spanked me, put me on punishment, etc., but nothing worked. My grandmother finally put her foot down and said "you are not getting another bicycle until you know how to take care of one". This was a hard but worthwhile lesson. I didn't get another bike for THREE YEARS! I was eight years old by the time I received another one. But when I got that new bike, I really cherished it. I washed it or wiped it down after every ride. I made sure to keep the chain oiled and the tires properly inflated. I learned to repair flat tires and do any required maintenance on that bike. I had that bike until I was almost eleven when an older kid stole it. It still looked new after almost three years!

I wasn't nearly as hard on my kids, but I made sure that they understood that whatever possessions the family had was worth taking care of. It was little things such as not writing on walls because this was our family's home and the family deserved to live someplace attractive and well maintained. Not throwing trash in and around our home. Picking up toys and putting them away after each use. Kids have to know about the consequences of their actions.

When my son was very young 3-4 years old, I had asked him on several occasions to pick up his toys when he was done because they were safety hazards. I came home one day and proceeded to step on toys and almost fell. So, I did what any good parent would do, I picked them up. I proceeded to throw them in the garbage.

Later on, my wife and my son were both furious with me, but I never had to remind him to pick up his toys again. Was this extreme? It probably was. The point I'm trying to make is that you must teach your children acceptable attitudes towards their possessions and that there are consequences for negligence.

The earlier you start the better! I'm not telling you to be a crazy parent, but you must set some type of boundaries and rules concerning both your and your children's possessions. Your kids *must* learn that life has consequences!

A former coworker told me about an incident that occurred with their child. This child had been disrespectful and acting out. The child's game console was taken away as punishment. After a few days, the child asked for the game console back. When the parent refused, the child proceeded to run out of the house with the game console in tow and proceeded to throw it into the middle of the road where it was promptly run over by a truck and destroyed.

My former coworker asked me what should they do? I told them that under no circumstances should they replace the game console which costs approximately $300 at the time of this writing and to seek professional help for their child. As this was not normal behavior for an eleven-year-old.

Parents remember that kids will act out. Yours will, mine did, and you did as a child. Everybody's kids are just kids. Normal healthy kids do act out occasionally. A parent's job is to set parameters for our children. If your children don't seem to be responding to anything, please seek professional help! In anger, you may feel like choking your kid like a chicken, but don't!!!

I know I spoke about this in an earlier chapter, but parents when you are feeling overwhelmed by the whole child-raising responsibilities please get some help. It's okay to get help. It is not a stigma to get professional help either when and if needed.

If and when you get children to respect both your possessions and their possessions at an early age, it makes the teenage years so much easier to bear. If possible, start early. If you already have teenagers that are not acting appropriately remember to get help. You don't have to be an island all by yourself.

18. Why History?

For both good and nil history influences us. This influence is both personal and cultural. History doesn't define us but can help explain why things are a certain way.

"History is an unending dialogue between the present and the past and the chief function of the historian is to master and understand the past as a key to understanding of present"

-CH Carr

History is another tool that can help strengthen and empower our children. Jews have used their sense of history and destiny coupled with *hard work* to overcome the horrific treatment of the 1930's Europe and the discrimination of the 1940s and 1950's America.

Contrary to the belief of some, the Jews weren't given anything. They went out and took the opportunity by the horns and shook success out of it. Even more so, Black people are not going to be given anything worthwhile either. It is futile to expect the government or anyone else to save you or help you.

We must look at every opportunity and squeeze every ounce of success from those opportunities. As such we must give our children historical examples of successful people who just happen to look like them. The quote "Success breeds Success" is true.

"We are not makers of history. We are made by history"

\- Dr. Martin Luther King Jr.

History gives us a sense of not just who we are, but also why we are. I was blessed to be alive in the late 1960's early 1970's. During this time there was constant ongoing academic study and mass media dialog concerning the diaspora of African Americans. As a teenager, the natural outgrowth of these discussions was to be pulled deeper and deeper into American history, African history, and African American history in particular.

This immersion into history caused a total paradigm shift of personal image and sense of self. It caused me to question my role in society as a whole. The study of history expanded my self-worth and gave me a feeling of belonging. At the time of this writing, the portrayal of African Americans in American media is uneven at best and often biased. To offset these negative ethnic and racial images the study of history is critical.

"A generation which ignores history has no past and no future."

- Robert Heinlein

The study of history made certain things seem very obvious to me. For instance, I stopped using the "N" word. Contrary to modern rhetoric, history shows that this word was never meant to be a term of endearment or anything but a mean nasty put down. Let's exclude this word from the lexicon once and for all. America, we don't need it!

Another obvious historical fact. Whether it was voluntary or forced, Black people helped build this country. As such we *belong* here! Our citizenship was born of blood, sweat, tears, and tragedy. Just like the phoenix we rose.

As parents, our only true job is to *grow* confident, successful, vibrant, and financially stable children. Just like flowers and plants, our children need to be nurtured. In order to do this, we must give our children the fertilizer of love and understanding. They must be watered from the spigot of education and spirit. They need to be placed in the soil of history and allowed to absorb the sunshine of possibilities. After all this, we need to allow them to grow.

"A small body of determined spirits fired by an unquenchable faith in their mission can alter the course of history."

- Mohandas (Mahatma) Gandhi

19. Pray, Pray, and Pray Some More

As we come to the end of this book, I want to remind you to get busy and not procrastinate. The writing of this book was a true labor of love. I've shared my experiences and observations on successful child-rearing backed by expert statistics and analysis. But, if you don't act on it, it was for naught.

We often hear that knowledge is power. But this statement is only a half-truth. Knowledge is only potential power. Knowledge is power only when put to use ----and then only when the use made of it is constructive.

\- David J. Schwartz, Ph.D.

The Magic of Thinking BIG

After you've raised a Successful Black child that the worrying doesn't end there. Even though both my children are adults now and earn well over $100,000 per year they are still my babies.

I thought that having them learn to drive was tough. Or when it was time for them to go away to college and I thought that I was going to lose my mind. Yet my wife and I survived.

Adulthood is a different challenge. When children reach adulthood, you will have much less control and input into their lives, but if you have been true to some of the principles laid out in this book, you'll maintain an open dialogue with them and they'll still come to you for advice. Remember no matter what, you have something that they lack - *Your Experience.*

Once you've done everything that you could there is nothing else to be done. If our adult children make decisions that we don't agree with, at the end of the day it's their lives. When our children are adults, no amount of arguing or berating them will work. This can and will strain your relationship with them.

Once our children are successful adults that have been educated, have prosperous careers and or running successful business' life should be good. If you step back and just let them enjoy their lives, you can enjoy it right along with them.

As parents, we reap huge benefits from having successful children and not just financial benefits. Even though the plane tickets, money, and vacations have been nice. The biggest benefit is the lack of drama and peace of mind. *Successful people just don't have time for silliness and drama, they are much too busy trying to enjoy life.*

I'll end here by thanking God! With his help, we were able to raise Successful Black Children here in America. Don't forget to Pray, Pray, and Pray some more for your children and grandchildren.

.

www.ingramcontent.com/pod-product-compliance
Lightning Source LLC
Chambersburg PA
CBHW071541040426
42452CB00008B/1081